𝔈𝔥𝔢 𝔊𝔯𝔢𝔞𝔱 𝔚𝔞𝔯, 1914-1919

THE
BOOK OF REMEMBRANCE

OF

THE 5ᵀᴴ BATTALION

(PRINCE ALBERT'S)

SOMERSET LIGHT INFANTRY

LONDON: PRIVATELY PRINTED AT THE CHISWICK PRESS

1930

THE ROLL OF HONOUR

THE 1/5TH BATTALION (PRINCE ALBERT'S) SOMERSET LIGHT INFANTRY

Pte.	ABBOTT, Albert	.. ..	Palestine	26.11.18
Pte.	ASHLEY, Walter John	.. .. ..	Palestine	23.11.17
Pte.	BAILEY, Matthias ..	.. .. ..	Palestine	22.4.18
Pte.	BARBER, Clifford	.. ..	Mesopotamia	24.1.16
Pte.	BARKER, Walter Harold ..	.. ..	Mesopotamia	31.12.17
Pte.	BARNES, Frederick Charles	.. ..	Palestine	23.11.17
Pte.	BAXTER, Harold	.. ..	Palestine	23.11.17
Pte.	BELLRINGER, Charles Henry	.. ..		
Pte.	BILLING, Charles	.. ..	Palestine	1.11.17
Pte.	BOND, Charles	.. ..	Palestine	1.5.18
Pte.	BOND, Thomas	.. ..	Palestine	23.11.17
Pte.	BOSLEY, William Charles ..	.. ..	Palestine	8.4.18
Pte.	BRAIN, John	.. ..	Palestine	23.11.17
Pte.	BRANCHFLOWER, Albert ..	.. ..	Palestine	25.9.18
Pte.	BROOMFIELD, Ernest William	.. ..	Palestine	10.4.18
Pte.	BROWN, Albert	.. ..	Palestine	15.12.18
Pte.	BRYANT, Charles	.. ..	Palestine	23.11.17
Pte.	BUCKLER, William Henry	.. ..	Palestine	23.11.18
Pte.	BURBAGE, Henry ..	.. .. ..	Palestine	9.1.18
Pte.	CARRUTHERS, Walter James	.. ..	Palestine	23.11.17
Pte.	CHANT, Percy	.. ..	India	25.9.15
Pte.	CHIDGEY, James	.. ..	Palestine	12.4.18
Pte.	CLARKE, Harold	.. ..	Mesopotamia	7.8.16
Pte.	COOPER, Henry	.. ..	Palestine	14.4.18
Pte.	COSNETT, George Henry ..	.. ..	Palestine	18.11.18
Pte.	COTTERELL, Ernest Edward	.. ..	Palestine	13.11.17
Pte.	COX, John ..	.. ..	Palestine	23.11.17
Pte.	CROCKER, William ..	.. .. ..	Palestine	15.4.18
Pte.	CURRY, John George	.. .. ..	Palestine	25.11.18

Pte.	Davey, William F.		Palestine	23.11.17
Pte.	Davis, Samuel		Palestine	12.4.18
Pte.	Dear, Archibald		Palestine	16.5.17
Pte.	Dunstan, William James		Palestine	10.4.18
Pte.	Fallon, William Michael		Palestine	10.4.18
Pte.	Farmer, Frederick		Palestine	1.5.18
Pte.	Follett, Henry		Mesopotamia	1.5.16
Pte.	Foxford, Arthur		Palestine	13.11.17
Pte.	Furse, Edward		Palestine	23.11.17
Pte.	Furse, Frederick		Palestine	26.11.17
Pte.	Gale, Orlando Tom		India	13.4.15
Pte.	Gardiner, Edwin Charles		Palestine	10.4.18
Pte.	Garrett, Charles		Mesopotamia	22.7.16
Pte.	Gear, Ernest		Palestine	5.9.18
Pte.	Gifford, Henry Ernest		Palestine	23.11.17
Pte.	Giles, Francis John		Mesopotamia	22.11.15
Pte.	Giles, Walter		Palestine	20.11.17
Pte.	Gill, Tom (2521)		Mesopotamia	8.7.16
Pte.	Gill, Tom (4316)		India	31.8.16
Pte.	Glover, Francis Edgar		Palestine	2.12.17
Pte.	Good, William		Palestine	19.9.18
Pte.	Govett, Percival George		Palestine	12.12.17
Pte.	Grabham, William Henry		Palestine	3.12.17
Pte.	Haines, William Henry		Palestine	26.12.17
Pte.	Hales, Charles		Palestine	23.11.17
Pte.	Hames, Wyndham		Palestine	10.4.18
Pte.	Harding, Henry		Palestine	27.7.18
Pte.	Harvey, Frederick		Palestine	23.11.17
Pte.	Hayes, Herbert		Palestine	23.11.17
Pte.	Haysham, Ernest		Palestine	22.11.17
Pte.	Haysham, Harry		Palestine	22.11.17
Pte.	Hensley, Richard		Palestine	23.11.17
Pte.	Hill, Albert		India	16.11.16
Pte.	Hill, Sidney		Mesopotamia	23.9.16
Pte.	Hopkins, Albert		Palestine	23.11.17
Pte.	Howard, Cyril		Palestine	23.11.17
Pte.	Howard, Edgar Thomas		Palestine	10.10.18

ROLL OF HONOUR

Pte.	Huish, Walter	Mesopotamia	28.7.16
Pte.	Iles, Henry Charles	Palestine	23.11.17
Pte.	Iley, Herbert John	Palestine	3.10.17
Pte.	Irish, Alfred	Mesopotamia	28.7.16
Pte.	Jeffrey, George	Palestine	23.11.17
Pte.	Jones, John	Palestine	14.5.18
Pte.	Jones, Leonard	Mesopotamia	14.7.16
Pte.	Kent, Arthur James	Palestine	24.10.18
Pte.	Kiddle, Edward John	Palestine	23.11.17
Pte.	King, Joseph	Mesopotamia	14.9.16
Pte.	King, William	Mesopotamia	28.4.17
Pte.	Knight, Walter	India	28.1.15
Pte.	Langton, Frank	Palestine	13.1.18
Pte.	Lowe, Fred	Palestine	7.12.18
Pte.	Luxton, Thomas	Palestine	23.11.17
Pte.	Lye, William	Palestine	23.11.17
Pte.	Marks, Ernest	Palestine	12.10.17
Pte.	Matthews, Arthur D. Taylor	Palestine	9.4.18
Pte.	Mears, Frederick William	Mesopotamia	25.11.16
Pte.	Milton, Charles	Palestine	23.11.17
Pte.	Milton, Clifford	India	1.11.15
Pte.	Milton, Edward	Palestine	23.11.17
Pte.	Mitchell, Earle	Palestine	23.11.17
Pte.	Mitchell, Ernest Edgar	Palestine	9.4.18
Pte.	Palmer, Harry	Palestine	23.11.17
Pte.	Parsons, Charles	India	17.5.16
Pte.	Pearse, William Ewart George	Palestine	10.4.18
Pte.	Peppin, Harold	Palestine	23.11.17
Pte.	Perrott, William James	Palestine	17.4.18
Pte.	Perry, William	Palestine	4.9.17
Pte.	Perryman, Frank Matthew	Palestine	10.4.18
Pte.	Poole, Arthur	Palestine	15.11.18
Pte.	Poole, Frederick	Palestine	23.11.17
Pte.	Porter, Edward John	India	4.12.16
Pte.	Raffil, Walter James	Palestine	23.11.17
Pte.	Rasell, William Oliver	Palestine	22.11.17
Pte.	Ritchie, James	Palestine	1.5.18

Pte.	ROBINSON, Thomas	.. .. ..	Palestine	11.4.18
Pte.	ROWE, George	.. .. ..	Palestine	13.11.17
Pte.	RUSHWORTH, Leslie	.. .. ..	Palestine	23.11.17
Pte.	RYALL, Herbert James	.. .. ..	Palestine	23.11.17
Pte.	SALTER, Frederick H.	.. .. ..	Mesopotamia	28.9.15
Pte.	SEAR, Thomas	.. .. ..	Palestine	3.9.17
Pte.	SHEPHERD, Albert Ernest	.. ..	Palestine	15.10.18
Pte.	SHORT, Charles	.. .. ..	Palestine	23.11.17
Pte.	SLADE, Stanley	.. .. ..	Palestine	23.11.17
Pte.	SMITH, Herbert Victor	.. .. ..	Palestine	4.12.17
Pte.	SMITH, John	.. .. ..	Palestine	19.9.18
Pte.	SMITH, Walter	.. .. ..	Palestine	22.11.17
Pte.	SOLOMON, William John	.. ..	England	16.10.18
Pte.	SOPER, Arthur	.. .. ..	Palestine	13.11.17
Pte.	SPENCER, Walter John	.. ..	Palestine	23.11.17
Pte.	STONE, Joseph Arthur	.. .. ..	Palestine	26.11.17
Pte.	STUCKEY, Frederick	.. .. ..	Mesopotamia	31.12.16
Pte.	STURGIS, Samuel Henry	.. ..	Palestine	12.4.18
Pte.	STYLE, Ambrose	.. .. ..	Palestine	23.1.18
Pte.	SULLY, Alfred	.. .. ..	Palestine	30.1.18
Pte.	SULLY, Leonard	.. .. ..	Mesopotamia	25.6.16
Pte.	SUMMERHAYES, Herbert	.. ..	Palestine	23.11.17
Pte.	TALBOT, Stanley George	.. ..	India	11.10.15
Pte.	TAYLOR, Amale Ralph	.. ..	Palestine	10.4.18
Pte.	TAYLOR, William	.. .. ..	Palestine	1.1.18
Pte.	THORNE, Albert	.. .. ..	Palestine	23.11.17
Pte.	TOOGOOD, William	.. .. ..	Palestine	25.11.17
Pte.	TROAKE, Ernest	.. .. ..	Mesopotamia	25.8.16
Pte.	TUCKER, Henry John	.. .. ..	India	1.7.15
Pte.	TURNER, Joseph	.. .. ..	Palestine	23.11.17
Pte.	VALLANCE, William Robert	.. ..	Palestine	22.11.17
Pte.	WARMAN, Archibald	.. .. ..	Palestine	23.11.17
Pte.	WARREN, William Charles	.. ..	Palestine	18.11.18
Pte.	WEBBER, William Francis	.. ..	Palestine	3.9.17
Pte.	WELLMAN, William Norman	.. ..	Palestine	11.4.18
Pte.	WESTERN, Frank	.. .. ..	Palestine	21.10.18
Pte.	WHITE, George	.. .. ..	India	3.2.17

ROLL OF HONOUR

Pte.	WILSON, George Herbert	Palestine	14.11.17
Pte.	WOOLLARD, William	Palestine	3.1.18
Pte.	WORRELL, Harry	Palestine	5.6.18
Pte.	YANDELL, Walter	Mesopotamia	31.5.16
L.-Cpl.	BARNARD, Joseph Edward	Palestine	22.11.17
L.-Cpl.	CHURCHILL, Robert	Palestine	9.12.17
L.-Cpl.	HOLT, Percy Lionel	Palestine	13.11.17
L.-Cpl.	LOCK, Mark	Palestine	22.11.17
L.-Cpl.	PENNY, Alfred Samuel	Mesopotamia	16.7.16
L.-Cpl.	THOMPSON, Fred	Mesopotamia	28.9.15
L.-Cpl.	WYATT, George	Palestine	10.4.18
Cpl.	CHAPMAN, William	India	2.5.15
Cpl.	DADE, Henry George	India	31.8.16
Cpl.	GALLEY, Douglas	Mesopotamia	7.10.16
Cpl.	GREEDY, William John	Palestine	10.4.18
Cpl.	HILL, John	Palestine	22.11.17
Cpl.	HOLLAND, Harry	Palestine	22.11.17
Cpl.	JENNINGS, Tom	Palestine	27.7.18
Cpl.	PARSONS, Hubert	Mesopotamia	13.4.16
Cpl.	PURCHASE, Wilfred S. E.	Palestine	20.11.17
Cpl.	SAUNDERS, William	Palestine	11.4.18
Cpl.	TOTTLE, Henry	Palestine	22.11.17
L.-Sgt.	TURNER, Clifford	Palestine	9.4.18
Sgt.	EDWARDS, Allan Cecil	Palestine	22.11.17
Sgt.	ENO, Frank Alfred	Palestine	23.11.17
Sgt.	ENO, Henry	Mesopotamia	10.12.15
Sgt.	FLOWER, Arthur Charles	Palestine	16.11.17
Sgt.	FOOTE, William	Palestine	22.11.17
Sgt.	GARDNER, William John	Palestine	6.10.17
Sgt.	HAYES, Charlie	Palestine	24.12.17
Sgt.	JENNINGS, Alfred Reginald	Palestine	8.10.18
Sgt.	REDDING, Henry	Palestine	23.11.17
Sgt.	SHUTTLE, William John	Palestine	22.11.17
Sgt.	STAGG, Albert Edward	Palestine	23.11.17

THE 2/5TH BATTALION (PRINCE ALBERT'S) SOMERSET LIGHT INFANTRY

Pte.	ADAMS, Albert	.. ..	Mesopotamia	18.6.16
Pte.	ADAMS, Arthur	.. ..	Mesopotamia	26.10.17
Pte.	BELLRINGER, Marcel	.. ..	Mesopotamia	21.12.15
Pte.	BINDING, Ernest William	.. .. ..	India	12.10.17
Pte.	BOARD, Fred	.. ..	Burma	25.1.15
Pte.	BROWN, Henry	.. ..	India	16.4.19
Pte.	CAREY, Charles Cyril	.. .. ..	Mesopotamia	26.1.17
Pte.	CARTWRIGHT, Thomas Bertram	.. ..	India	31.5.18
Pte.	COATES, Frank Ronald	.. .. ..	India	22.6.18
Pte.	COLLARD, Ivan James	.. .. ..	India	1.4.18
Pte.	CRIDLAND, Ernest	.. ..	Burma	17.8.15
Pte.	CRUICKSHANK, Alexander	.. ..	Mesopotamia	26.11.15
Pte.	DOWDING, Jesse	.. ..	India	9.11.17
Pte.	DOWNTON, Herbert	.. ..	Burma	21.3.17
Pte.	ELFORD, George William	.. .. ..	India	4.3.16
Pte.	FOOKS, P.	.. ..	India	16.8.19
Pte.	FUDGE, Henry Charles	.. .. ..	India	30.5.17
Pte.	GAYLOR, F.	.. ..	India	29.11.18
Pte.	GIBBS, Ernest	.. ..	Egypt	23.11.17
Pte.	HUTCHINGS, Charles	.. .. ..	Burma	23.7.16
Pte.	JENNINGS, Charles	.. ..	Mesopotamia	25.4.16
Pte.	LONG, Charles	.. ..	Mesopotamia	28.11.15
Pte.	MORGAN, Reginald	.. ..	Mesopotamia	9.10.16
Pte.	PARKER, Ernest Albert	.. .. ..	India	21.10.18
Pte.	PEACOCK, T.	.. ..	Aden	2.1.19
Pte.	POPE, F.	.. ..	India	27.8.19
Pte.	PIPE, Norman	.. ..	Mesopotamia	31.12.16
Pte.	RICHARDS, J.	.. ..	India	30.6.19

ROLL OF HONOUR

Pte.	Rowden, Mansel	Burma	26.5.16
Pte.	Saunders, Frederick	India	20.7.18
Pte.	Smith, E.	India	25.7.18
Pte.	Taylor, Thomas	Mesopotamia	21.12.15
Pte.	Tancock, Stanley John	Mesopotamia	8.3.16
Pte.	Turner, Robert	Mesopotamia	12.8.16
Pte.	Webber, Harry	India	22.1.19
Pte.	Wellman, Bert	Mesopotamia	22.11.15
Pte.	Westcott, Albert	Burma	24.12.15
Pte.	Wheadon, George	Mesopotamia	8.2.16
Pte.	Williams, Ernest Charles	At Sea	24.12.14
Pte.	Young, William	India	23.11.17
L.-Cpl.	Frost, Clifford	India	27.10.18
Cpl.	Adams, John	Burma	23.8.17
Cpl.	Mahrenholz, Ferdinand Edmund	India	29.8.17
Cpl.	Parminter, Robert	Burma	11.6.15
Cpl.	Parsons, Hubert	Mesopotamia	13.4.16
Cpl.	Simpson, Archibald	Mesopotamia	15.7.16
Cpl.	Weaver, Henry William	India	21.10.17
Sgt.	Frampton, Thomas John	India	10.5.19
Sgt.	Pattimore, Charles	India	26.8.17
C.Q.M.S.	Dyer, Roy	Mesopotamia	4.10.18
C.S.M.	Pilton, Frederick George	India	24.5.18

THE 5TH BATTALION (PRINCE ALBERT'S) SOMERSET LIGHT INFANTRY

Pte.	BAKER, Ernest	.. ..	England	16.4.15
Pte.	BESLEY, Thomas ..	.. .. ..	England	16.2.15
Pte.	FOSTER, Edward ..	.. .. ..	England	21.12.14
Pte.	LEE, Arthur	.. ..	England	7.12.14
Pte.	ROBERTS, Samuel ..	.. .. ..	England	4.10.14
Pte.	STREET, William Frank ..	.. ..	England	4.10.14
Pte.	WARREN, Sidney Charles ..	.. ..	England	28.1.15
L.-Cpl.	CURREY, Joslin William ..	.. ..	England	28.6.15
L.-Cpl.	DENCH, Reginald Percy ..	.. ..	England	22.1.17
Sgt.	WOOLCOTT, John Albert ..	.. ..	England	19.1.17

ROLL OF HONOUR

2nd Lt.	ELLIOTT, H. W.	Palestine	13.11.17
2nd Lt.	GOULD, E. W.	Palestine	11.4.18
2nd Lt.	HANNAFORD, W. A.	Palestine	23.11.17
2nd Lt.	MALONEY, D.	Palestine	10.4.18
2nd Lt.	RUSSELL, H. R.		
Lieut.	COOK, C. S. B.	France	15.9.16
Lieut.	CRISP, C. B.	France	16.8.17
Lieut.	HARRIS, C. St. J.	England	10.9.15
Lieut.	JOWERS, J. F.	France	24.3.18
Lieut.	REID-HARDING, C. H.	Palestine	15.2.18
Lieut.	STALEY, F. C.	Mesopotamia	8.3.16
Capt.	ARNOLD, G. F.	Mesopotamia	8.3.16
Capt.	BANES-WALKER, G.	Palestine	22.11.17
Capt.	MAJOR, A. O.	Palestine	23.11.17
Capt.	RIDDELL, R. C. H.	N.W. Frontier	14.1.20
Capt.	SPRING, E.	England	16.8.24
Major	BRUTTON, R. H.	India	15.1.16

CONTENTS

CHAP. | | PAGE
INTRODUCTORY CHAPTER 1

1/5TH BATTALION

FOREWORD by Brigadier-General LORD ROUNDWAY, C.M.G., D.S.O., M.V.O. 7
I. MOBILIZATION TO EMBARKATION 11
II. INDIA 14
III. THE MESOPOTAMIA DRAFTS, 1915-1916 22
IV. EGYPT AND PALESTINE 34
V. ARMISTICE TO RETURN OF CADRE TO TAUNTON 65
HONOURS AND REWARDS 73
MAP OF MESOPOTAMIA 76
MAP OF PALESTINE 77

2/5TH BATTALION

FOREWORD by Major-General SIR HERBERT A. RAITT, K.C.I.E., C.B. . 79
I. FORMATION 81
II. BURMA 83
III. THE MESOPOTAMIA DRAFTS 89
IV. INDIA 100
V. DISBANDMENT 109
HONOURS AND REWARDS 112

EPILOGUE by Colonel J. W. GIFFORD, V.D. 113
ROLL OF OFFICERS FROM 1920 ONWARDS 115

INTRODUCTORY CHAPTER

THE 5th Battalion (Prince Albert's) Somerset Light Infantry was formed under the Territorial and Reserve Forces Act, 1907, from the 2nd and 3rd Volunteer Battalions, Somerset Light Infantry, and came into being in April 1908. The Battalion established its Headquarters at Taunton, with detachments at Pitminster and Bishops Lydeard, and the first Commanding Officer was Colonel W. Marsh, V.D.

Other Companies were formed at Williton (with detachments at Minehead, Watchet, and Washford), Bridgwater, Burnham (with a detachment at Langport), Yeovil, Crewkerne, Wellington (with detachments at Milverton and Wiveliscombe), and Chard.

It may be interesting, especially to those officers and men who joined the Battalion in its early days, to set out the following Battalion Order by Colonel W. Marsh, V.D., dated 11th April 1908:

The Commanding Officer desires on the transfer of the Battalion to the Territorial Army, to thank all ranks for the services they have so generously and patriotically given in the past.

He greatly regrets that the new organization will bring about a loss to the Battalion of some men who have passed the age limit prescribed by the Army Council. He earnestly hopes that the same patriotic spirit which has done so much for the Battalion in the past will continue to prevail, so that all ranks, not precluded by the age limit, will become members of the Territorial Army. He is confident that the conditions of service will not in any instances be felt hard or pressing, and that the hearty co-operation of employers of labour will be given to the Military Forces.

He observes with much satisfaction that in many parts of the County attestation is proceeding rapidly and with great enthusiasm, and it is his great wish that the men of the old 2nd Volunteer Battalion Somerset Light Infantry should show themselves second to none in their patriotic desire to serve their King and Country.

(*Signed*) H. F. HARDMAN,
Captain and Adjutant.

A return of the strength of the Battalion on 30th April 1908 was as follows: officers 22, other ranks 469. These figures had been increased in 1912 to 22 officers and 820 other ranks, and in 1913 the return recorded was 24 officers and 796 other ranks.

It is not within the province of this history to write extensively of the Battalion and its activities in the years before the Great War, but it may be of general interest to record the fact that Colours were presented to the Battalion in June 1909 by His Majesty King Edward VII, on the West Lawn, Windsor Castle.

The Colour Party was under the command of Major J. R. Paull, and the other officers on parade were Captain E. B. Kite, Captain F. D. Urwick, Lieut. W. H. Bradford—who had the honour of carrying the King's Colour—Lieut. R. E. Gifford—who had the honour of carrying the Regimental Colour—Lieut. A. O. Major, Sergeant-Major T. Bond, and a representative party of 13 other ranks.

This was the first occasion in history of Colours being carried by a Territorial Unit, and the Colour Party, when they returned to Taunton the same evening, were met by Headquarters Company and the Regimental Band. The streets were crowded and the Colours were received with great enthusiasm by the West Country people. The following are details of Camps, Commands, and Appointments during the years 1908-14:

Places of Annual Training in Camp

Weymouth	1908
Windmill Hill, Salisbury Plain	1909
West Down South, Salisbury Plain	1910
Bovington, Wool, Dorset	1911
Parkhouse, Salisbury Plain	1912
Woodbury Common, Exmouth	1913
Bulford, Salisbury Plain	1914

Commanding Officers

Colonel W. Marsh, V.D.	1.4.1908 to 18.9.1909
Colonel E. Trevor, V.D.	19.9.1909 to 18.7.1910
Lieut.-Colonel J. W. Gifford, V.D.	19.7.1910 to 3.1.1913
Lieut.-Colonel E. F. Cooke-Hurle	4.1.1913 and throughout the Great War.

Adjutants

Captain H. F. Hardman, S.L.I.	1.4.1908 to 22.7.1909
Captain L. E. C. Worthington-Wilmer, S.L.I.	23.7.1909 to 15.9.1910
Captain L. A. Jones-Mortimer, S.L.I.	16.9.1910 to 31.12.1913
Captain T. A. Walsh, S.L.I.	1.1.1914 to 9.10.1914

Quartermasters

Hon. Captain E. Willie	1.4.1908 to 13.8.1913
Hon. Lieut. T. Bond	14.8.1913 and throughout the Great War.

THE HISTORY

OF THE

1/5TH BATTALION (PRINCE ALBERT'S) SOMERSET LIGHT INFANTRY

WRITTEN AND COMPILED BY

MAJOR E. S. GOODLAND, M.C.

AND

CAPTAIN H. L. MILSOM

1930

FOREWORD

AS I recall the splendid achievements of the Battalion, certain scenes come vividly before me.

A typical Egyptian night, two officers, the Commandant of the Imperial School of Instruction, Zeitoun, and his Adjutant, were standing at the quiet siding at Helmieh waiting for the arrival of the 1/5th Battalion the Somerset Light Infantry. Punctual to the moment, like a snake the huge troop train glided in; one whistle, and the war strength Battalion detrained, and in ten minutes, headed by their bugles and band, they marched off. The Adjutant turned and said: " As good as a Regular Battalion. You are lucky, Sir." I echoed his sentiments. I was aware that the 1/5th Battalion was to form part of the newly formed 233rd Infantry Brigade, which I had been selected to command. That night was the beginning of a friendship which was to outlive the War.

Many hard months of training followed. Eventually the Battalion found themselves in the Apex, and shortly afterwards were ordered to raid the " Old British Trenches." Many unsuccessful raids had been attempted, and it was left to the 1/5th Somerset Light Infantry to show the Army of Palestine how to do it. Wonderfully organized and gallantly led, success was assured. G.H.Q., Divisions, Brigades, vied with each other to be the first to congratulate the Battalion on achieving what was thought to be impossible.

Think for a moment what the work you did that night meant to the *morale* of the newly formed 75th Division.

More weeks of training, and then the most wonderful advance which any Army has ever known. On the night, 6th-7th November, " Over the Top," followed on the 13th by the splendid fight at Mesmiyeh when the Battalion added to its laurels by taking the village and advancing to a further position a mile to the north. A day's so-called rest. Then the great achievement, the taking of the Pass of Beth-Horon and of Enab village, at the top of the Pass. How well I remember seeing the 1/5th Somerset Light Infantry on the right of the road, the 1/4th Wilts, their great sister Battalion on the left, column of Companies in extended order flying into the misty rain; then the bugles sounding the Battalion Call, announcing that Enab had been taken—more prisoners but few casualties. The honour of capturing Jerusalem was denied, the Key to the City, Nebi Samwil, had yet to be dealt with. This was taken the following night by the 3/3rd Gurkhas, and most gallantly they held on to it. The next day saw the hopeless attack on El Jib, a fortified village. I had asked for time for reconnaissance and to get our guns up. Supported only by three mountain guns, the Brigade Group of six Battalions was ordered to attack; they were hurled back. The following day the same result with fearful casualties; short of rations and ill-clothed for the time of year. It took two fresh and well-fed Divisions, supported by all their gun power, to capture El Jib.

The scene changes, the 233rd Brigade marching back down the Pass of Beth-Horon: strength, as far as I recollect, 17 officers, including Brigade H.Q., and 813 other ranks, the 1/5th Somerset Light Infantry in rear, the post of honour, as indomitable as ever.

More frequently in the line than out, a long, dreary, wet winter was passed: discipline never relaxed.

In the spring you were chosen to find the Guard of Honour for H.R.H. the Duke of Connaught, the Colonel of my own Regiment. I was very proud of the show you put up on 11th March 1918, and prouder still of the few words with which His Royal Highness privately greeted me, expressing his entire approval of the Guard.

Jellalabad Day saw the next phase of your activities. The attack of Rafat and Arara, a well conceived and gallantly carried out attack—to my mind one of the most brilliant achievements in the record of the Battalion—a true representation of the tenacity of the men of Somerset.

A further long period of watching and waiting.

FOREWORD

Watching for THE DAY—the day which the Army of Palestine, knowing their Chief, realized must come to pass.

And the day came, 18th-19th September. Nothing could withstand the gallant charge of your men: it was left to other Units to finish the work. That dawn saw the end of the fighting as far as you were concerned.

The winter of 1918-19 was comfortably spent at Kantara. While the Battalion was awaiting final demobilization, a sudden order came to proceed to "Minieh area" to quell the native rising. Your discipline carried you through this period, perhaps the most trying weeks of your overseas service.

In Lieut.-Colonel E. F. Cooke-Hurle, D.S.O., the Battalion had a Commanding Officer second to none, a fearless leader, a great gentleman, beloved by all ranks. By his untimely death in the hunting field I lost a great personal friend.

Gentlemen, you have written a splendid and most vivid History to be handed down to posterity.

I thank you for the privilege which you have accorded me in asking me to write this foreword.

Roundway.

Brigadier-General.[1]

[1] Formerly Brigadier-General The Hon. E. M. Colston, C.M.G., D.S.O., M.V.O., Commanding the 233rd Brigade, E.E.F.

CHAPTER I

MOBILIZATION TO EMBARKATION

AT the outbreak of War on 4th August 1914 the 5th Battalion Somerset Light Infantry was stationed at Sling Plantation, Bulford, on Salisbury Plain, having gone into Camp for the annual training on the 25th July. The strength of the Battalion was then 20 officers and 789 other ranks.

On the declaration of War the Battalion received the order to mobilize and to proceed to temporary War Stations at Plymouth, where on arrival on the morning of the 5th August it was distributed as follows:

Headquarters and " A " Company were established at Laira Battery, " B " and " D " Companies at Laira Schools, " C," " G," and " H " Companies at Prince Rock Schools, " E " Company at Hardwick's Farm and Plympton Schools, and " F " Company at Plymstock Schools and Dunstone Plantation, and the machine guns were sited for the defence of Long Bridge.

The arrival of Special Reserve Battalions in Plymouth released the 5th Battalion to return on the 9th August to Salisbury Plain, and the Battalion entrained at Devonport in the early hours of the morning, and finally reached Durrington Camp after a long and tiring march from Salisbury. The Battalion, together with the 4th Battalion Somerset Light Infantry, the 4th Battalion Dorsetshire Regiment, and the 4th Battalion Wiltshire Regiment, now formed the South-Western Infantry Brigade—under the command of Colonel G. S. McD. Elliott—of the famous Wessex Division, which, commanded by Major-General C. G. Donald, C.B., was destined shortly to proceed overseas, though nothing was then known of any future movements.

The time at Durrington Camp was occupied with the finding of guards for the supply depot at Fargo and for the Netheravon Flying School, the instruction of newly joined officers and men, and with preparations for the anticipated further expansion of the strength of the Battalion.

Selected officers were despatched to the various Company areas in Somerset to conduct a Recruiting Campaign. The success of their efforts is indicated by the fact that no less than 916 recruits had joined the Battalion by 14th September. Scenes of great enthusiasm marked the arrival of these reinforcements in Camp.

The Battalion was fortunate in having as its Commanding Officer one who had seen much service with the Regiment, and whose influence in the County was considerable. To Lieut.-Colonel E. F. Cooke-Hurle the Battalion owes a great debt for his invaluable services at this critical time, when experienced guidance and leadership meant everything. Splendidly too was he backed by the Adjutant, Captain T. A. Walsh of the 2nd Battalion.

A considerable extra strain was thrown upon the organization and administration of the Battalion by this sudden increase in the strength, and credit is due in no small measure to the energy and ability of the Quartermaster, Lieut. T. Bond, that the arrangements for the additional accommodation and equipment were carried out so smoothly.

On 17th September Camp was moved to West Down South—the strength of the Battalion then being 34 officers and 1912 other ranks. It was on this same day that authority was given to raise second line units.

Accordingly orders were issued for the formation of a Reserve Battalion, the following officers being appointed as a nucleus of the 5th Battalion Somerset Light Infantry Reserve Battalion—Major J. R. Paull (Commanding), Captain W. T. Burridge, and Captain C. H. Goodland.

It was generally understood that the first line Battalions would be called upon shortly for service abroad, and although this obligation did not at that time extend to the Territorial Army, yet volunteers were not wanting for service overseas. On the contrary so great was the response that the necessary numbers were immediately completed and some hundreds had to submit to disappointment.

The two Battalions remained together at West Down South, but were independent for drill and administrative purposes. It may be here mentioned that from now onwards the two units were kept entirely separate—one ultimately forming the 1/5th and the other the 2/5th Battalion.

Towards the end of September the whole of the Wessex Division, of which the 1/5th Battalion formed part, received orders to proceed to India. Major-General C. G. Donald, the G.O.C. of the Division, conveyed a message from Lord Kitchener, the Secretary of State for War, which was issued in the following form:

" The Division being one of the first to volunteer for General Service as a whole, had been selected for the very important work of garrisoning India. Although they may be disappointed at not going on Active Service immediately, they were rendering an equally great service to the Empire. If the War were a protracted one they would be relieved by their Reserve Battalions and brought back for Active Service. In any case they should return to England before the final completion of the War, so that they should suffer no disadvantage in the rush for employment.

They were going to the finest training ground in the world, and must take every opportunity to render themselves fit to meet any emergency.

It was also pointed out that by undertaking this Imperial obligation nothing would be lost; the troops would be brought back at the end of six months, and would share in all honours equally with those proceeding to France. A temporary break in the narrative may here be made to acknowledge that force of circumstances prevented these promises from being fulfilled. The men of Wessex rendered their obligation in the spirit of a duty, rather than in the letter of a bargain. On Thursday the 8th October the Division was drawn up for an inspection by Lord Kitchener, who wished to review the Division before it proceeded overseas. After a prolonged wait, however, it was announced that urgent State affairs had necessitated the cancellation of the Review. Lord Kitchener's messages, as given above, were then conveyed to the Division. The strength of the 1/5th Battalion, which was, hitherto, 1,000 strong, had now to be reduced to 800 in order to conform to the Field Service Strength of a British Infantry Battalion in India. On the 9th October the Battalion marched out of Camp at 8 a.m. and entrained at Amesbury for Southampton—the port of Embarkation. The officers proceeding overseas were:

Lieut.-Colonel E. F. Cooke-Hurle (*Commanding*); Major R. H. Brutton; Major E. B. Kite; Captain D. S. Watson; Captain F. D. Urwick; Captain R. E. Gifford; Captain H. Bradford; Captain A. O. Major; Captain G. F. Arnold; Captain A. S. Timms; Captain J. Duke; Captain F. H. F. Calway (*Adjutant*); Lieut. C. C. H. Hawken; Lieut. C. F. L. Ruck; Lieut. F. C. Staley; Lieut. J. H. Blake; Lieut. G. W. Rawlings; 2nd Lieut. E. S. Goodland; 2nd Lieut. A. L. Blake; 2nd Lieut. E. A. H. Churchill; 2nd Lieut. H. Vaughan-Jones; 2nd Lieut. G. Banes-Walker; 2nd Lieut. H. L. Milsom; 2nd Lieut. G. P. Pavey; 2nd Lieut. A. H. Virgin; 2nd Lieut. D. H. G. McCririck; 2nd Lieut. T. Moore; 2nd Lieut. R. B. Moore; Lieut. and Quartermaster T. Bond; Captain C. F. Murphy, R.A.M.C. (*T.F.*).

CHAPTER II

INDIA

ON arrival at the docks the Battalion embarked on the H.T. "Alnwick Castle," but as there was insufficient accommodation on board for all the officers, Major R. H. Brutton and Major E. B. Kite, together with the subalterns, were transferred to the H.T. "Kenilworth Castle." This was the flagship of a fleet, comprising many ships, conveying the entire Wessex Division overseas, and at dawn of the 9th October the convoy put to sea.

Two British cruisers accompanied the transports as far as Gibraltar, where on 14th October, with signals of farewell and good luck, they turned back, leaving the convoy to be escorted hence by the French battleships "St. Louis" and "Charlemagne." At this stage of hostilities, submarine warfare had not developed to any appreciable extent outside the North Sea, and little or no danger was anticipated from that source, though interference might have been expected from marauding raiders such as the German cruiser "Emden"—then at large and regarded as a considerable menace. Malta was reached on the 18th October, and Port Said on Thursday the 22nd.

The entrance of the convoy into the Suez Canal was an occasion which may well claim to be of an historical interest, for this was the first time a British Force, composed entirely of Territorials, had sailed East of Suez in the service of the Empire. The significance of the fact must have been in the minds of all who witnessed the event, which was rendered the more impressive by the exchange of salutes effected between the transports and the French Battleships as they passed one another. The "Alnwick Castle" at the head of the convoy, led the way through the Canal and thus fell to the 1/5th Battalion Somerset Light Infantry the unique distinction of being the first Territorial Battalion on Imperial duty bound, to enter that famous Canal which links the West with the East.

Much time was to pass, many hardships to be endured, and many lives to be laid down before that duty was destined to be fulfilled; for it was not until five momentous years and more had gone by that a small cadre—a faint shadow of

INDIA

this same Battalion—was free to re-pass, homeward bound, with this duty honourably done.

Suez was reached on Friday the 23rd October and here the convoy anchored for four days.

The monotony of the stay at Suez was relieved by sports, bathing, and boat races, and officers and senior N.C.O.s were given permission to land. On 27th October the convoy weighed anchor and set off again. In the Red Sea the temperature rose perceptibly and the heat proved very trying, especially to the troops crowded between decks; every effort was made and various devices used to catch the breeze and ventilate the ships.

Other convoys, one of British troops and another of Australian—westward bound—were passed during the voyage out.

A brief stay was made at Aden on 2nd November, and after a very calm and uneventful voyage across the Indian Ocean, the convoy reached Bombay on the afternoon of 9th November; the troops disembarked the following day.

Before leaving Salisbury Plain an announcement had been made that on arrival in India the Battalion would proceed to Jhansi, but at Bombay orders were received to entrain for Jubbulpore—less one Company which would be stationed at Nagpur. Accordingly " C " Company, under the command of Captain D. S. Watson, was detailed as the Nagpur detachment and reached that Station on 12th November. The Battalion detrained at Jubbulpore the same day, and there received a very cordial reception. The band of the Cheshire Regiment—who were then being relieved for active service with the British Expeditionary Force—played the Battalion into Barracks.

The arrival of fresh troops from England to replace Regular Units under orders for service in France, obviously caused some considerable interest in India, especially in the native mind, which was profoundly impressed by the might of Britain and her ability to maintain her strength in the East, and at the same time throw large forces into France. Enemy activity and propaganda had made every endeavour to bring about an upheaval in India, and the landing of the Wessex Division undoubtedly relieved a critical situation.

The time at Jubbulpore was occupied in getting into shape again after the comparatively idle conditions enforced by the voyage—fitting out with khaki drill, medical inspections, and generally settling down to the usual routine of Indian Army life.

The debt the Battalion owed to Lieut.-Colonel Cooke-Hurle for his skilful guidance and care in the initial and critical stages of training in England has already been acknowledged—but a further tribute to his memory is due for his invaluable services at this particular period, when his previous experience of service in the East was a tremendous asset to the Battalion. Captain F. H. F. Calway had succeeded to the post of Adjutant, and his loyal and untiring services at this time, and during the whole period of his appointment, are deserving of the highest commendation. Mention, too, should be made again of the Quartermaster, Lieut. T. Bond, who also had seen much service in India, and whose knowledge of the commissariat routine was of the greatest help.

It so happened that the 2nd Battalion Somerset Light Infantry were stationed at Quetta throughout the War, and it was arranged for them to send their No. 1 Company to Nagpur, and their No. 2 Company to Jubbulpore to give demonstrations to the 1/5th Battalion, and they remained for a month. This arrangement was of the utmost service to the Battalion, and special praise is due to the officers, N.C.O.s, and men of these two Companies for the instruction and assistance thus afforded. One of the main duties at Jubbulpore was the posting of an officers' guard over the Gun Carriage Factory, a mile or so outside the station. But the stay at Jubbulpore was not to be of very long duration, for on the 4th December the 4th Battalion Royal West Kents relieved the Battalion, which entrained at noon the next day. After picking up the Nagpur detachment en route and breaking the journey at Gwalior, where H.H. The Maharajah Scindia of Gwalior most kindly entertained the Battalion—the new station, Ambala, was reached on the morning of 7th December. Conditions now became more stabilized as far as the Battalion was concerned. It appeared evident that no early move from Ambala was probable, and strenuous training commenced in earnest. One Company was detailed for the Movable Column—a force formed for emergency purposes and held in readiness to proceed to any area of disturbance at a moment's notice. In addition the Battalion was included in the No. 1 Mobile Brigade of the Internal Defence Scheme.

Early in 1915 orders were received that the progress of training should be tested by the famous standard laid down by Lord Kitchener, when Commander-in-Chief in India, and known as " Kitchener's Test." This meant three very strenuous days, during which the Battalion, being provided with necessary supplies and transport, had to fend for itself. The first day, after a fifteen mile march, an attack was made with ball ammunition on a prepared objective. The attack over, outposts were found and a bivouac formed for the night. The following day a retiring action was fought and finally a night march had to be carried out. Although the Test was interrupted on this occasion by a terrific thunderstorm, which made all transport impossible, the ordeal was successfully endured and the Battalion emerged with credit.

On the 20th April came the first call to provide a detachment for active service, and the good news sent a thrill of excitement through the Battalion. It transpired that orders had been received to furnish a Draft of one subaltern, one sergeant, one corporal, two lance-corporals, and twenty-five men for service with Indian Expeditionary Force " D," operating in the Persian Gulf. Competition for inclusion in this select band was naturally extremely keen, and volunteers were not wanting. Finally the honour of the command fell upon Lieut. E. S. Goodland, and on the 13th May 1915 he and a party of picked N.C.O.s and men marched out of Barracks amidst the enthusiastic cheers of their less fortunate comrades, to join the 2nd Battalion the Dorset Regiment at Basrah. A detailed account of the experiences of this Draft is set out in Chapter III following.

Up to the time of the departure of this Draft (May 1915) the Battalion had held to the old Eight Company system. But a change was now made and the Battalion reorganized in Double Companies, as follows:

Old Company System	Double Company System
" A " Capt. G. F. Arnold " B " Capt. A. S. Timms	" A " Major E. B. Kite
" E " Capt. W. H. Bradford " F " Capt. F. D. Urwick	" B " Major F. D. Urwick
" G " Capt. R. E. Gifford " H " Capt. J. Duke	" C " Capt. R. E. Gifford
" C " Capt. D. S. Watson " D " Capt. A. O. Major	" D " Major D. S. Watson

On the whole the Battalion withstood the first experience of a " hot weather " on the Plains very well, but it was a great relief to all ranks to be moved in July to the Hills, and to take over duties at Dagshai in place of the 1/4th Dorsets.

The official Diary makes very little note of the course of events at Dagshai and, indeed, there is nothing much to record. One of the chief duties was to provide an officers' guard for the Military Prison, wherein a large number of native sowars were under arrest upon a charge of sedition, and awaiting a Court Martial. Ultimately many of these sowars were found guilty and condemned to death, after which the prisoners were transferred by road and rail under a guard of two officers and some fifty men to the Prison at Ambala, where the sentences were carried out.

Much of the time at Dagshai was devoted to special training in Hill Warfare. The Gurkha Battalions stationed at Solon and Sabathu lent valuable assistance by co-operating in these particular exercises.

On 1st August 1915 a further call was made on the Battalion to provide yet another Draft of one corporal, one lance-corporal, and thirteen men for the 2nd Dorsets. This Draft left Dagshai on 13th August, embarked at Karachi on 19th August, and ultimately joined their comrades of the first Draft in Mesopotamia, and their experiences are also incorporated in Chapter III following.

The Battalion left Dagshai on 2nd November, and marched in two stages to Chandigarh, where it remained under canvas until 1st December, for the purpose of Battalion training. On the latter date a three days' march back to Ambala was started. Shortly after arrival at Ambala, the Battalion was asked to nominate a subaltern, willing and fit for active service with the Indian Expeditionary Force " D." Lieut. F. C. Staley, who up to this time had been the Battalion Machine Gun Officer, volunteered, and left the Battalion on 17th December. He became attached to the Oxford and Bucks Light Infantry in Mesopotamia and was appointed Machine Gun Officer to the 28th Brigade. During the fighting which took place early in March, for the relief of Kut, he was killed in action, and by his death the Battalion lost a very keen and efficient officer. At about the same time in December Capt. G. F. Arnold was sent to the 2/5th Somerset Light Infantry in Burma, to take over signalling course duties, and was ultimately transferred to the 31st Divisional Signalling Company and joined General Aylmer's Force in Mesopotamia. He too was killed in action on or about the 8th March, in the Dujaila Redoubt operations. The news of the deaths of these two gallant officers and of the other N.C.O.s and men who had been killed in Mesopotamia during the advance to Ctesiphon, and the retirement to Kut, was received by all ranks with the deepest regret.

During the year 2nd Lieuts. W. G. Bradford, N. Whitley, and A. L. Price joined, and the following officers left the Battalion:

Capt. W. H. Bradford took up a Staff Appointment. Lieut. J. H. Blake also took a Staff Appointment, but rejoined the Battalion towards the end of 1916. Lieut. C. C. Hawken was invalided to England; Lieut. C. F. L. Ruck and Lieut. E. A. H. Churchill went to Signal Companies. 2nd Lieuts. G. P. Pavey and D. H. G. McCririck were appointed to the 2nd Battalion (P.A.) Somerset Light Infantry. 2nd Lieut. H. Vaughan-Jones joined the Indian Army.

INDIA

A sad event occurred early in the New Year to cast a gloom over the Battalion, for on 15th January Major R. H. Brutton, T.D. Second in Command, succumbed to an attack of pernicious malaria. Major Brutton joined the 2nd V.B. Somerset Light Infantry on the 4th May 1895, and so had had nearly twenty-one years' service with the Battalion. He was a friend to all ranks and his loss was keenly felt; he was buried with full military honours at Ambala Cemetery.

The months of January and February were spent in carrying out Field Operations of an extensive kind, and another " Kitchener's Test " was completed with credit.

In March it became apparent that a change of station was contemplated, and on the 20th of the month the Battalion, having been relieved by the 1/7th Hants Regiment, left Ambala for Meerut.

Early in May a Draft of 9 officers and 449 N.C.O.s and men arrived from England. The officers were: Capt. W. T. Burridge, 2nd Lieut. G. P. Clarke, 2nd Lieut. S. H. Elder, 2nd Lieut. E. Spring, 2nd Lieut. V. W. Helps, 2nd Lieut. L. J. Hennesey, 2nd Lieut. A. S. W. Evans, 2nd Lieut. A. M. Foster, 2nd Lieut. C. H. R. Harding.

During the hot weather of 1916 the Battalion was divided: Battalion Headquarters with " C " and " D " Companies were stationed at Chakrata in the Hills, whilst " A " and " B " Companies remained at Meerut under the command of Major E. B. Kite. The greater part of the time was devoted to the training of the recruits of the Draft. The season being exceptionally wet in the Hills, very little was done other than this. It was not until October that any event of general interest to the Battalion occurred worthy of note. Orders were then received to despatch a Draft to reinforce the 1/4th Battalion Somerset Light Infantry in Mesopotamia. Accordingly on the 20th, Capt. R. E. Gifford, Lieut. L. J. Hennesey and 150 N.C.O.s and men left Meerut and sailed from Bombay on the 24th, and their movements and experiences are set out in Chapter III following.

Headquarters and the two Companies hitherto stationed at Chakrata now returned to Meerut, and on the 22nd the Battalion was once more reunited. On the 15th November the Battalion left Meerut, and marched, via Delhi (where it bivouacked for the night under the Fort) to Tughlakabad, for the concentration of the 43rd Infantry Brigade. A whole month was given up to Brigade training, after which the Battalion returned to Meerut.

Although no mention has been made as yet in this history regarding the

Battalion's prowess in sport, yet this side of Regimental activities was by no means neglected. The usual inter-company contests in Cricket, Association and Rugby Football, took place at intervals. But it was in the cold weather of 1916 that the 1/5th Somersets gained their highest honour in sport when the Battalion Rugby team, captained by 2nd Lieut. G. P. Clarke, captured the " Rugby Union Challenge Cup " at Calcutta.

The strength of the Battalion on 31st December 1916 was 30 officers and 948 N.C.O.s and men. In addition to the officers joining during the year who have already been mentioned, 2nd Lieut. G. F. Bunning, and 2nd Lieut. C. G. Ames arrived from England.

Lieut. G. N. Rawlings left the Battalion to join the Supply and Transport Corps. Lieut. A. H. Virgin also joined the Indian Army. Lieut. A. L. Blake was transferred to a Signal Company, and ultimately saw service in Mesopotamia with the 35th Infantry Brigade and took part in the operations leading to the final capture of Kut and the march on Baghdad.

Towards the end of the year an intimation had been received that the Battalion would shortly move towards the N.W. Frontier, to take part in manœuvres on an extensive scale. Accordingly, on 13th January, an Advance Party, consisting of Lieuts. E. S. Goodland and R. B. Moore, with 100 N.C.O.s and men, was sent forward to prepare camp at Pir Gumat Shah, near Burhan, which is situated between Attock and Rawal Pindi. It transpired that the 1/5th Somerset Light Infantry, together with the 1/9th Middlesex Regiment, 1/4th Wilts Regiment, and a Gurkha Battalion, were to complete the 43rd Infantry Brigade, which formed part of the 16th Indian Division, concentrated for significant reasons at Burhan. This was the largest force that had been collected near the Frontier up to this period of the War, and was fully equipped in every respect for up-to-date operations.

On 26th January the Battalion reached Pir Gumat Shah and found that the Advance Party had prepared an excellent camp in complete readiness for occupation. During the first part of the stay at Burhan the time was occupied mostly in Battalion, and occasionally in Brigade, training. Divisional manœuvres commenced in March, and on the 2nd the Battalion carried out a long and rather tiring march of twenty-two miles to Jhang. This march was made the more trying on account of the very poor quality of the road, which was merely an excessively dusty track. The spirits of the Battalion, however, were exceptionally high at this time, because of persistent and promising rumours of a call for active service. Although many Drafts had been despatched overseas, yet the Battalion

INDIA

very naturally yearned for a chance of going on service as a whole. Many times during the stay in India hopes had risen, only to be doomed to disappointment. Now, however, it did seem as if the longed-for summons was really at hand, and expectations were strong. Actually on 6th March orders were received to be prepared to move overseas at short notice. Those who were present on that memorable occasion can never forget the tremendous enthusiasm this glad news aroused.

The following day the Battalion marched back from Jhang to the standing camp, and such were the buoyant spirits of all ranks that the march was accomplished in record time. It did not take long to complete all preparations for complying with the order for readiness—exactly four days, in fact. But it was not until the 26th that the Battalion was allowed to entrain at Burhan for the long journey to Poona, *en route* for Bombay. Some little time, however, was to be spent at Poona making final preparations. All rifles were handed in at the Arsenal, and advantage was taken of the chance to get all ranks inoculated against enteric and para-typhoid.

On the night of the 25th April the Battalion left Poona and arrived at the Alexandra Docks, Bombay, the following morning. Embarkation took place at once, and 17 officers and 838 other ranks went aboard the Transport "Chakdara." (The 11 remaining officers, for whom there was no room on the Transport, left the next day by the P. & O. ship "Malwa" for Suez.) At one o'clock p.m. the "Chakdara" slowly left the Dock with ringing cheers from the men of the 1/5th Somerset Light Infantry aboard, answered enthusiastically by the crowds ashore. It was a great send-off and those officers who—being temporarily left behind—witnessed the occasion had every reason to be proud of their Battalion, more especially as the Embarkation Officer was heard to remark: "There goes the best and cheeriest crowd we have yet sent off." Truly a fitting valediction!

And so ended the two and a half years' stay of the 1/5th Somerset Light Infantry in India. Personnel had changed considerably during that period (of the original 30 officers and 800 Warrant officers, N.C.O.s and men who landed in India in November 1914, only 15 officers and 441 Warrant officers, N.C.O.s and men embarked on the 26th April 1917), but the spirit remained the same. A constant drain had gone on the whole time; Drafts to Mesopotamia, officers and men to special services, such as signalling units, etc., "time expired" men and those medically unfit for active service, had all sapped the strength. But the Drafts sent out to replace these losses quickly and adequately filled the gaps and thus the Battalion left India a first-class fighting unit, its garrison duty nobly done, and sterner work ahead.

CHAPTER III*

THE MESOPOTAMIA DRAFTS, 1915

IT has been recorded in the preceding chapter that the first Draft for Mesopotamia left the Battalion at Ambala on 13th May 1915, and the full list of the personnel was as follows:

Lieut. E. S. Goodland, Sergeant H. Eno, Corporal W. Foote, Lance-Corporal H. Parsons, Lance-Corporal A. V. Nichols, Private W. Yandle, Private F. W. Mears, Private F. Salter, Private W. Pillar, Private C. Barbour, Private W. King, Private J. King, Private J. W. T. Colsey, Private E. M. Taylor, Private H. Clarke, Private F. J. Giles, Private G. Rowe, Private W. Russell, Private T. Fone, Private W. Bryant, Private F. Stuckey, Private R. Hatcher, Private E. W. Hill, Private E. Troake, Private T. Gill, Private C. Best, Private W. Huish, Private C. Garrett, Private F. Thompson, Private A. Irish.

The troop train contained similar Drafts from other first line Territorial Battalions, *en route* to Mesopotamia, some of which were also destined for the 2nd Battalion Dorset Regiment.

At Mooltan there was a few hours' halt and rest, and here further Drafts joined the train.

And now began the journey across the Sind Desert to Karachi. This in itself is somewhat of an adventure, but in the middle of May, in a crowded troop-train with no ice or any special protection against the terrific heat, it was a most unpleasant experience, and it was little short of a miracle that there were no casualties amongst the men of the Draft.

Four days were spent at a rest camp at Karachi and eventually the Draft embarked on 20th May. The voyage across the Persian Gulf passed without any special incident, but immediately the troopship passed the bar at the head of the Gulf, and entered the Shatt al Arab, the journey became intensely interesting. At Fao, where the original British Force made its landing on 6th November 1914, the first signs of War were seen, and on proceeding up the river several armed Turkish launches, which had been sunk by the British gunboats, were passed.

Basrah was finally reached on 26th May, and the Draft disembarked and

* Reference map on page 76.

THE MESOPOTAMIA DRAFTS, 1915

marched to the Headquarters of the 2nd Battalion Dorset Regiment, who were in camp on the outskirts of the town.

The reception the officers and men of this famous Regular Battalion extended to their Territorial reinforcements was remarkable in its warmth and cordiality. At the landing at Fao, and throughout the advance during December 1914 to Basrah, the Dorsets had seen much fighting—they were, moreover, heavily engaged in the Battle of Shaiba on 14th April 1915, and played a brilliant part in that decisive victory, but they had suffered many casualties in officers and men, and their ranks were sadly depleted. It is, therefore, not to be wondered at that the men of the 1/5th Somerset Light Infantry, and those of the other Territorial units, were greeted with open arms.

Basrah, at the time of the arrival of the Draft, was a scene of indescribable activity, for it had been decided to clear the Turks from Lower Mesopotamia, and to proceed up the Tigris and capture Amarah, and preparations for the advance were being carried out with the greatest energy. The operations were to be under the command of Major-General C. V. Townshend, C.B., D.S.O., who had recently arrived from India to command the 6th Division.

At this time, May 1915, the most advanced position held by the British Force was Qurnah, which was captured in December 1914. Standing at the junction of the Euphrates and Tigris, forty miles up stream from Basrah, it was a position of considerable strategic importance. According to a popular Mohamedan fiction, it was the site of the Garden of Eden, but in reality it was a collection of filthy lanes and mud and reed hovels, with a few brick houses, barracks, and a custom house, and it was left in a dreadful condition by the Turks. During the British occupation much sarcasm was expended on its Eden-like qualities.

The Turkish main positions were approximately four to five miles northward of Qurnah, astride the Tigris, and as at this time of year the river was in full flood, all these positions were surrounded by water. The Infantry employed in the first phase of the attack were to be placed in "bellums"—the native flat-bottom boats—and had undergone intensive training in the propelling and manipulation of these unwieldy craft. The attack was to be supported by the Naval Flotilla and guns, and machine guns were mounted on horse-boats, mahailas, rafts, and every conceivable craft the country could produce. This collection became known in the force as "Townshend's Regatta."

It had been decided to start the operations on the 31st May, and at dawn the advance commenced. The 2nd Dorsets, which included the Draft of the 1/5th Somerset Light Infantry, formed a unit of the 16th Brigade, under Brig.-General

W. S. Delamain, C.B., D.S.O., and on the first day proceeded up the Tigris in a steamer in support of the 17th Brigade, who carried out the attack in " bellums."

By 7.30 a.m. the attack had developed according to plans and it was here the Draft came under enemy gunfire for the first time in the War, for the Turkish Artillery concentrated on the Naval Flotilla as the steamers proceeded up the river. Meanwhile the " bellum " attack was so successful that the advanced enemy positions had been captured without serious loss, and the 17th Brigade was re-forming for a further attack. The Turks had sustained many casualties in killed and wounded, and had lost several hundred prisoners.

The first phase of the operation had, therefore, met with complete and unexpectedly easy success, and the 16th Brigade, who had had a wonderful view of the fighting throughout the morning, were not called upon to go into action.

Orders were now issued for the continuance of operations on the following day, 1st June, and to the 16th Brigade was allotted the task of capturing the Turkish main position at Abu Aran. At dawn the convoy steamed up the river, preceded by armed mine-sweepers, and the 16th Brigade, with the 2nd Dorsets leading, made a landing at Abu Aran under cover of the guns of the Naval Flotilla.

There was no enemy opposition and it was eventually found that all positions had been evacuated by the enemy who were fleeing northward in every available craft, and the 2nd Dorsets arrived in time only to fire at the last boatload of retreating Turks.

For the next few days the men of the Draft of the 1/5th Somerset Light Infantry participated in the pursuit of the enemy up the Tigris until Amarah was reached. The story of this pursuit—the exploits of the ships of the Naval Flotilla, the sinking of the numerous Turkish gunboats, the capture of hundreds of prisoners and immense quantities of stores and ammunition—will always remain one of the most amazing episodes of the Mesopotamian campaign. The culminating point was reached when the armed mine-sweeping launch " Shaitan," which had outdistanced the other ships, captured Amarah single-handed and with great daring, for her total crew only consisted of one officer and eight sailors.

The rest of the flotilla and General Townshend arrived at Amarah soon after mid-day and formally accepted its surrender. The Union Jack was hoisted and arrangements made to secure the town with the very small force available. This, excluding the few officers, amounted to a total of only forty-one men. Fortunately, the night passed quietly, but early on 4th June the Arabs, beginning to realize the British weakness, commenced to loot and to make an attack from the west, but happily the troops of the 16th and 17th Brigades began to arrive at about 6.30 a.m. and were just in time to avert a probable disaster, and during the afternoon the situation became quite secure.

Amarah, whose occupation was now complete, was found to be a town of pleasing appearance and of some commercial importance, containing some ten to twelve thousand inhabitants. It was located at the Tigris end of a main trade route to Persia and provided fairly good quarters for the Force, except during the hottest weather.

The combined naval and military operations of the four days, 31st May to 3rd June, had been a brilliant success. The men of the Draft, without being seriously engaged in the fighting, had endured the hardships of campaigning and the discomforts of the intense heat with splendid spirit, and had emerged from their first taste of active service with the greatest credit.

The Turks on the Tigris line had eventually retired to a position in front of Kut, and for some weeks the British, at and around Amarah, were chiefly occupied in outpost duty, and in closely watching the Arab tribes in the neighbourhood, whose friendship was extremely fickle. The men of the Draft were kept fully occupied with a great deal of night duty and several were evacuated to hospital with fever and dysentery. During August preparations were begun for a further advance up the river and, on 1st September, the British Force was concentrated at Ali Gharbi, a distance of fifty miles by land, and eighty miles by water, above Amarah. During this time the Turks were pushing down stream detachments of troops from their main army at Kut, but these fell back without serious opposition, and by 16th September the Force, with the 2nd Dorsets and the Draft with the advanced troops, had reached Sanniyat, about eight miles from the Turkish positions, The Naval Flotilla and river transports had accompanied the advance, and the Draft, with the other Infantry, had marched along the river bank. It was intensely hot by day with an average temperature of 110° to 120° in the shade, and the men who were heavily laden suffered very much from exhaustion and exposure to the sun.

By 26th September the concentration at Sanniyat was completed and preparations for the great attack were made. The Turkish position on both sides of the river ran along the Es Sinn banks in front of Kut and after months of careful preparation was very formidable, extending on the right bank southwards for about five miles, and on the left bank northwards for about seven miles. The enemy had, moreover, blocked the Tigris close to their position with a boom, constructed of barges and cables, and commanded at close range from both banks of the river by guns and fire trenches.

It must here be recorded that during the concentration at Sanniyat the second Draft of two N.C.O.s and thirteen men, which had left the 1/5th Battalion Somerset Light Infantry at Dagshai on 13th August, reached the attacking Force and marched into the bivouac of the 2nd Dorsets. As may be imagined, they were given a very warm welcome by the members of the first Draft—there were many tales to be told—Battalion friendships were renewed—comradeship established again and henceforth the men of the two Drafts settled down together to play their part side by side in the coming operations. The nominal roll of this Draft is as follows:

Corporal D. Gally, Lance-Corporal A. S. Penny, Private H. Barker, Private L. Jones, Private L. Sully, Private L. Moore, Private J. T. Osborne, Private G. Priddle, Private J. Moody, Private H. Follett, Private A. J. Hawker, Private J. W. Davis, Private C. H. Bellringer, Private W. H. Hook, Private W. R. Frampton.

On 26th-27th September a further advance was made to Nukhailat, four miles from the Turkish position. It had then been decided to launch the British attack on the left bank of the river, but in order to deceive the enemy a large force, in which the Drafts were included, was sent along the right bank, and here much display was made; all available tents were pitched and a great deal of obvious trench digging was carried out.

On the night of the 27th-28th September, however, practically the whole of this force crossed to the left bank of the Tigris in readiness for the decisive battle fixed for the 28th. The main idea in the attack was to envelope the left flank of the hostile position and afterwards to swing round southwards to the river, and to the 2nd Dorsets was allotted the task of making a frontal attack on Centre Redoubt, under the personal direction of the G.O.C. the 16th Brigade, General Delamain.

It was here the men of the Drafts had their first experience of serious night operations. Marching throughout the night the position of deployment was reached about 5 a.m., and when the sun rose, just after 6 o'clock, the troops were deployed and ready for the attack. It was a tedious business waiting for developments on either flank, and the 2nd Dorsets came under very heavy hostile artillery fire, but at 8.30 the order came for the advance. From the outset the British lines of Infantry met with a stout resistance from the entrenched enemy, but the attack was steadily pressed over the open and coverless plain; being well supported by artillery fire, the men of the 1/5th Somerset Light Infantry, with their comrades of the 2nd Dorsets, displayed great dash and determination, although suffering considerable casualties, and pushed on with extraordinary gallantry. Centre Redoubt was carried at the point of the bayonet at 10 a.m. and one hundred and thirty-five Turkish soldiers surrendered.

The men in the attacking line were reorganized in the positions won, but very soon heavy and confused fighting ensued, and the Turks, rallying well, started to counter attack.

The dust and the mirage had now made close artillery support difficult, but about midday the advance was resumed with great success until 3.30 p.m. By this time the men's exhaustion had become complete—they had been marching or fighting almost continuously since 2 a.m. and the heat, dust, and lack of drinking water had all contributed towards their fatigue.

After about an hour's rest, however, the men of the Drafts were called upon for a further effort, as another advance was ordered against strong hostile reinforcements, which had appeared moving from the southwards. Though dead beat and parched with thirst the men responded gallantly to the call upon them, and carried out the necessary deployment and extension skilfully and rapidly. Well supported by artillery the lines of British infantry made straight for the enemy with fine dash and spirit, and the Turks took up a defensive position along a dry canal and opened a heavy rifle fire supported by four field guns and two machine guns. In this attack the men of the Drafts were in the leading lines of the Dorset Regiment, and the advance led through long grass straight into the face of the setting sun, and there was some difficulty in finding out exactly where the enemy were making their stand. Scarcely halting to fire, however, and fixing bayonets at about four hundred yards distance, the men swept on and drove the enemy headlong from the canal. The Turkish losses were heavy, including their four guns, but they were saved from further destruction by the fall of night, which enabled the remnants of their force to make good their escape. The men were now so exhausted as to be incapable of further movement; they, therefore, occupied the enemy's position which had just been so gallantly won, where a fairly quiet night was passed.

It was an anxious moment when daylight came the next morning, the 29th September, but to everyone's intense delight the news soon arrived that the Turks, during the night, had evacuated all their positions east of Kut and were in full retreat up the Tigris towards Baghdad. Part of the British Force immediately started to carry out the pursuit of the enemy by river, but the men of the Drafts formed part of the force which marched in to occupy Kut, and also to clear up the battle-field and help to evacuate the wounded.

The men of the 1/5 Somerset Light Infantry had earned a high reputation during these operations; they had fought with the greatest gallantry and had endured the hardships and privations with splendid spirit. Unfortunately, there were casualties to record, for Private Salter and Private Thompson were killed at Centre Redoubt, and the following were wounded: Private Frampton, Private Rowe, Private Priddle, Private Hatcher, Private Russell, Private Best, Private Davis.

It was, however, remarkable that under the circumstances the casualties were so comparatively slight.

The river column pursued the Turks with as much speed as possible and on 5th October reached Aziziyah, 61 miles by land and 102 miles by river above Kut; news was there received that the Turks had halted and were installed in the already entrenched position at Ctesiphon.

Another general concentration at Aziziyah was ordered, and the men of the Drafts marched up from Kut with the other units of the 16th Brigade, and joined up with the advanced troops on 9th October. There were now several weeks of inactivity and the completion of the concentration was delayed owing to lack of river transports and aeroplanes, and to the prevalence of the Shamal (the seasonal northerly gales). It was therefore not until 21st November that General Townshend finally issued his orders for the battle of Ctesiphon, which was to take place the following day. The new Turkish positions were as usual astride the Tigris, and on the left bank, on which side the operations were to take place, extended northwards for about six miles, and consisted of fifteen closed redoubts along a line of low mounds, connected by a continuous trench, while at the extreme northern end were two strong redoubts known as Vital Point or V.P. The scheme for the British attack was practically a repetition of the successful one carried out at the Battle of Kut, namely, to envelop and turn the enemy's left flank, and for this purpose the force was divided into three columns, " A," " B," and " C "—" C " column for the frontal preparatory attack, " B " column for the flank attack, " A " column for the decisive attack on V.P.

The men of the Drafts formed part of the latter column which moved out towards evening on 21st November to its position of assembly, and as the sun set about 5 o'clock the Arch of Ctesiphon was seen by the force, standing out clearly against the blood red sky. As daylight broke on 22nd November the din of battle commenced with the opening of fire from the guns of the Naval Flotilla, and soon the men of the 1/5th Somerset Light Infantry were advancing towards V.P. with column " A." Proceeding at first in artillery formation, the advance was carried out continuously and rapidly until about one thousand yards from the enemy's position, when the Infantry came under heavy Turkish rifle and machine gun fire, which caused their lines to form into extended order, and the advance was then carried on in rushes of one hundred yards or so, the men only halting to take breath.

The leading lines were brought to a standstill by wire entanglements some forty yards in front of the hostile trenches, but the men were not to be deterred, and making their way through this obstacle by degrees, though not without heavy loss, they captured V.P. about 10 a.m. and the Turks, who had suffered heavy casualties, fled in disorder from the northern end of their line.

In recording this exploit in which the men of the Drafts were engaged, the official history of the Mesopotamia Campaign states: " the capture of V.P. was a fine performance, well conceived and gallantly executed; the operation is one of which the attacking force may well be proud."

Elsewhere the attack was proceeding with more or less success, but the British casualties had been very heavy and all reserves had been used up in capturing the enemy's first lines of defence. Moreover, strong Turkish reinforcements could be seen advancing to strengthen their line south of V.P. During the afternoon General Delamain collected as many men of his Brigade as possible, including the few men of the 1/5th Somerset Light Infantry who were not already casualties, and personally led an attempt to capture the Turkish second line, but after making some progress, a strong enemy attack in several lines could be seen moving forward on the left front, and further advance was impossible. At nightfall the depleted ranks of the British Force moved back to the Turkish first line of trenches, but only a handful of the men of the Drafts eventually reached the shelter of V.P. in the capture of which that morning they had played so gallant a part.

On this day Private Giles was killed and the following were wounded: Lance-Corporal Penny, Private Hawkes, Private Osborne, Private Moody, Private Taylor, Private Colsey, Private Bellringer, Private Hook, and it was learned afterwards that several of these had died of their wounds during the journey to the Base Hospitals.

When daylight broke on 23rd November it was possible to appreciate the condition of the British force. Men and animals were thoroughly exhausted and suffering from lack of water; units were much disorganized owing to the way they were intermingled in the previous day's fighting, and it was ascertained that the British casualties during the first day's operations, had amounted to over 4,500 officers, N.C.O.s, and men. It was, therefore, decided not to resume the offensive for the moment and this seemed to give the enemy encouragement, for during the afternoon the Turks launched an attack and made a determined effort to recapture their first line trenches. In this the enemy did not succeed and must have lost very heavily, but during the evening he made a further attempt, and from 9 p.m. onwards throughout the night the Turkish Army made six furious attacks on the British line, all of which were repulsed. On 24th November General Townshend came to the conclusion that the Turks had been largely reinforced, and that he would shortly be again attacked by superior numbers, and as his force was too weak to engage in another battle against such odds and force its way into Baghdad, he decided to fall back on his ships at Lajj, under cover of darkness.

All the world knows that it was ultimately decided to retire to Kut, and for the few remaining members of the Drafts of the 1/5th Somerset Light Infantry, the next few days were little short of a nightmare. For seven days and nights there was continual marching, rear-guard fighting and temporary trench digging, frequently without sufficient food or water, and often without sleep, but always under pressure from the enemy.

On 3rd December Kut at long last was reached and the enemy had been temporarily shaken off, but there was very little respite for the tired men, for there was much work to be done by the Garrison on the defences of the town.

The strenuous operations just described had cost the Drafts of the 1/5th Somerset Light Infantry dearly in killed, wounded, and sick. Lieut. E. S. Goodland had been evacuated to Basrah, and ultimately rejoined his Battalion in India, and as far as can be ascertained only 3 N.C.O.s and 14 men remained to undergo the trials and hardships of the siege of Kut.

The Turkish Army very soon closed in on Kut, and meanwhile the British Garrison were working night and day in order to make their position more secure. During 7th December there were increasing signs of enemy activity, and on the 8th, 9th, and 10th December the town was heavily and continuously shelled. On this last day the Turks made a determined attack to get a footing in Kut, but they were beaten off. It was during this attack that Sergeant Eno was killed, and his death cast a gloom over the remaining men of the Drafts. He had been through all the operations from Qurnah upwards and had made many friends in the 2nd Dorsets. He had proved himself a great fighter and a fearless leader, and was awarded a posthumous D.C.M. for conspicuous bravery and devotion to duty at the battles of Es-Sinn and Ctesiphon.

On 24th December the Turks made their most serious and sustained effort to carry the defences of Kut by assault, and on this day Private Stuckey was killed. Again and again the Turkish Infantry advanced with their bombers, sometimes actually entering the Fort and the British first line trenches, only to be ejected with heavy losses. Throughout the day furious hand to hand fighting took place, and the enemy did not relax their fruitless efforts until well into the night. Christmas Day dawned on a definite Turkish repulse, and, as it turned out, on their last serious attempt to take Kut by assault.

It is interesting here to record an extract from notes made by Private Taylor, almost the sole survivor of the men of the 1/5th Somerset Drafts. " We arrived at Kut played out, dropped where we halted and promptly went off to sleep. Next day started to dig trenches and were sniped by enemy continually—many being killed before trenches were deep enough to shelter us. Took it all rather as a joke to begin with and longed for Johnny Turk to have the unusual experience of getting *us* out of trenches—promised him a warm time—but it was no joke later on when food got scarce. Seemed to spend most of siege digging and pumping out water from trenches and looking for food, and used to cook all sorts of green stuff we found in the grass and even came down to eating mulberry leaves. Our 'baccy consisted of dried lime leaves and dried tea leaves. We found the horse and mule flesh jolly good stuff, but towards the end of the siege we were so weak, however, that we could hardly stand up. We could have fired our rifles all right, of course, but I don't think we could have done any bayonet fighting."

It was evident, during the early days of 1916, that the enemy had decided upon a period of comparative inactivity, and although there was constant shelling and sniping, the main policy was undoubtedly to be one of starving the British Garrison into submission.

In January 1916 the relief force started its advance from Ali Gharbi and the besieged men, already stricken with disease and with the ogre of hunger staring them in the face, were continually looking eastwards for the flash of the British guns. Days passed to weeks and weeks to months and time after time the relieving force hurled itself at the Turkish positions guarding Kut, but with little success. Equally unsuccessful, too, were the attempts to help the Kut garrison by dropping rations and medical comforts into the town from aeroplanes, the historic night march and attack on the Dujaila Redoubt, and finally the heroic adventure of the steamer Julnar in its endeavour to break through the boom with 270 tons of provisions for the beleaguered men.

On 26th April, when there was no food left and little chance of early relief, the position was so hopeless that General Townshend opened negotiation with the Commander of the Turkish Forces for surrender, and on 29th April the gallant garrison were forced to accept terms which amounted to unconditional surrender followed by captivity.

When the British Force passed out of Kut into Turkish hands, as far as is known, there were only 2 N.C.O.s and 7 men remaining of the 1/5th Somerset Drafts who were not already casualties, and of these only two, Lance-Corporal A. V. Nichols and Private E. M. Taylor, were alive at the time of the Armistice to return to England. The dreadful experiences of the Kut survivors are indescribable; they were marched to Baghdad, where they were paraded through crowded streets for hours, the Arab soldiery freely using sticks and whips to flog the stragglers on.

Without food or water, and many in rags and without boots, they were packed in railway trucks for seventy miles to Samarrah, there to begin their march of 500 miles across the desert to Asia Minor. Broken in health, but not in spirits, the Somerset men faced this terrible ordeal with stout hearts, but it proved too much for many of them, and they died of privation, neglect, and starvation before their destination was reached. In his notes Lance-Corporal A. V. Nichols writes: " we were driven in flocks like sheep right across Turkey. I think for about two months we were marched across deserts and wastes. Those of us who could sell anything to buy food, managed to get through but others didn't. The Turks and Arabs were terribly cruel and if a man was unable to get along he was beaten and left to die. For the two and a half years we were prisoners we worked for the Germans on the roads and railways."

Thus ends the story of the men of the Drafts who left the Battalion in India in 1915, such happy warriors, and it may be truly said of them that they had played their part nobly and well.

THE MESOPOTAMIA DRAFT, 1916

It will be remembered that the third and largest Draft for Mesopotamia left the Battalion at Meerut on 20th October 1916. The Draft, which consisted of Capt. R. E. Gifford, Lieut. L. J. Hennesey, and 150 picked N.C.O.s and men, sailed from Bombay on the 24th and ultimately joined the 1/4th Battalion Somerset Light Infantry, who were in camp at Shaiba on the outskirts of Basrah. Unfortunately, at this time the 1/4th Somersets were suffering from an epidemic of beri-beri and for six months were isolated and unfit for active operations, and this prevented the Battalion taking part in the final successful assault of Kut, and the march on Baghdad. In April 1917, the Draft forming part of the 1/4th Somerset Light Infantry, moved to Nasiriyah on the Euphrates, and there spent twelve uneventful months, except for occasional demonstrations when unfriendly Arabs became restive or quarrelled among themselves. In March 1918 the 1/4th Somersets returned to Basrah, and after an interesting trip up the Tigris arrived at Baghdad on 13th March, and after spending three or four days at Khirr Camp, marched to Hillah, just south of Babylon of ancient history. Part of the Battalion in which the Draft was included, was then almost immediately despatched some thirty miles south into the desert to take part in the blockade of Najaf, the Holy City of the Shiah Mohamedans. Owing to German and Syrian intrigue, there had been trouble in the neighbourhood of Najaf, resulting in the murder of a British Political officer, but beyond sniping from the city walls and occasional wild rifle firing by hostile Arabs, there was little resistance, and the blockade was raised on 4th May, and for some months afterwards the 1/4th Somersets remained to garrison the town.

The summer of 1918 passed, and was chiefly occupied in guard duties and ordinary routine work, and in October the Battalion moved by train from Baghdad to Tekrit; but the hope of the men of the Draft that they would take part in the final round-up of the Turks was not fulfilled, only those who happened to belong to the Lewis gun detachments participating in the crushing defeat of the enemy.

When the Armistice came the men were chiefly employed in the work of extending the railway, but shortly afterwards the Battalion again moved down to Baghdad and thence proceeded up the Diyalah River to Qizil Robat, near the Persian Frontier, and here a few months afterwards demobilization began, and soon the men of the Draft were on their way home to England.

Although, unlike their comrades of the two Drafts of 1915, these officers and men were denied the glory of participating in any outstanding action against the Turkish Forces, yet the duties they were called upon to perform were none the less essential and important.

During the two and a half years they spent in Mesopotamia, the physique, the efficiency, and the discipline of this Draft were often remarked upon and admired, and they remained always a credit to the 1/5th Battalion Somerset Light Infantry, which trained them and fitted them for active service, and whose offspring they were.

CHAPTER IV*

EGYPT AND PALESTINE

THE voyage from Bombay to Suez was uneventful. The sea was calm the whole way, and the health and spirits of the men were excellent. The convoy had sailed from India under secret orders and it was not until the transports were well out to sea that the Battalion knew that it was destined to join the Egyptian Expeditionary Force in Palestine. Aden was reached on 6th May, and Suez on the early morning of 11th May. The Battalion disembarked and entrained the same day, reaching Zeitoun, Cairo, at 10.30 p.m.

On the night of arrival, the Battalion was placed under canvas, but the following day was moved into an old " Prisoners of War " Hut Encampment under isolation orders, owing to a case of smallpox contracted on the voyage from Bombay. The quarantine restrictions were, however, soon removed, vaccination was carried out extensively in the Battalion, and all ranks were given an opportunity of visiting Cairo and the Pyramids, and other places of interest in the neighbourhood.

And now began another busy time of refitting and reorganization. As the Battalion left India entirely without arms and equipment, it was necessary for it to be completely fitted out on a War footing, and the next three weeks were occupied mainly in drawing new arms and equipment, transport and stores. The rifles issued were the short M.L.E. Mark III* for Mark VII ammunition, and every man fired twenty rounds at various ranges to become acquainted with the higher charge, the unit hitherto having only used Mark VI ammunition. The equipment drawn was leather with web packs which seemed unfamiliar to the Battalion after wearing the 1908 pattern web equipment since 1910. A Transport section was formed under the command of Lieut. T. Moore, and the animals issued, both chargers and mules, were a great improvement on those of India.

Unofficial information was received that the 1/5th Battalion was to join the 233rd Infantry Brigade of the 75th Division, and definite orders came sooner than anticipated, for on 3rd June, Headquarters 233rd Infantry Brigade under Brigadier-General the Hon. E. M. Colston, D.S.O., M.V.O., the 2/4th Hampshire

* Reference map on page 77.

Regiment, and the 1/5th Battalion Somerset Light Infantry, left Zeitoun for El Arish. 12 officers and 71 other ranks were left behind at Zeitoun, attached to the Imperial School of Instruction for various courses of training, *e.g.*, Lewis gun, bombing, etc.

The Battalion proceeded in two trains to Kantara where it detrained, crossed the Suez Canal to Kantara East Station, and there entrained again on the newly built Military Railway, *en route* for Palestine. The rolling-stock provided consisted of the ordinary open goods trucks, into which thirty men were packed with equipment and kits, and the journey was, therefore, extremely uncomfortable, but the Battalion was fortunate to make the journey to El Arish by train, and thus be saved the long weary marches over the desert, or on the improvised wire netting roads, which had fallen to the lot of the troops who had fought their way across the Sinai Peninsula.

The Battalion arrived at its camp at El Arish in the early morning of 4th June, and training was proceeded with. The camp was situated on sand-hills, and the men for the first few days found the soft sand very trying; the First Line Transport was constantly in difficulties, ten mules in some instances being required for even light loads. The training carried out was mainly route marching, and the practice of artillery formations and the attack. Each Company also carried out a certain amount of trench digging in connection with the El Arish defences, and the sandy ground in which the trenches were situated had to be revetted throughout with sandbags. The water supply in the Sinai Desert was somewhat limited, but all ranks thoroughly enjoyed the excellent sea bathing which El Arish provided.

On the 18th June orders were received to proceed with Headquarters 233rd Infantry Brigade and the 2/4th Hampshire Regiment to Rafa, and this move was made by train on 20th June. All the animals and First Line Transport carried out the journey by road, under Lieut. T. Moore's command, a distance of thirty miles.

It may here be of interest to recall the fact that throughout the remainder of the War, and indeed up to the time of the return of the cadre to England in 1920, the Battalion always formed one of the Units of the 233rd Brigade. The Brigade was commanded throughout by Brigadier-General the Hon. E. M. Colston,[1] D.S.O., M.V.O., himself a West countryman, who had already greatly distinguished himself on service in France. Under General Colston's guidance the Units in his Brigade were brought to a very high state of efficiency during the

[1] Afterwards Brigadier-General Lord Roundway, C.M.G., D.S.O., M.V.O.

months of training prior to the taking over of front line trenches. In the Battalion he became a very popular figure, and a staunch friend, and to his untiring devotion the Brigade owed a very great debt, and the 1/5th Battalion Somerset Light Infantry acknowledges that debt very gratefully.

The day after arrival at Rafa the Right Sector Defences were taken over from the 1/101st Grenadiers (I.A.), and on the same day the Battalion became responsible for six Blockhouses on the Sheik Quran Railway and a post at Kilo 207 on the Belah Railway. On the 29th June, however, the Battalion was completely relieved of all defence duties by the Alwar Infantry (Indian Imperial Service Troops).

The Battalion, which was inspected by the G.O.C., 75th Division, Major-General P. C. Palin, C.B., C.M.G., I.A., remained at Rafa for two months, carrying out intensive Brigade training, and periodically certain garrison duties, but an occasional visit from enemy aircraft served as a reminder that hostile forces were not far off; also there existed a necessity for some vigilance on the right flank in case of a surprise attack from Arab tribesmen, co-operating with the Turks. In order to increase the efficiency of the Battalion, a constant stream of officers, N.C.O.s and men proceeded to Schools of Instruction at Zeitoun and El Arish, and during this period Lieuts. H. W. Elliott, A. J. B. Coradine, and W. A. Hannaford, and 27 other ranks, joined as reinforcements from England.

On 11th August Nos. 1 and 4 companies, under the command of Major D. S. Watson, were despatched to the newly formed G.H.Q. camp near Kilo 207, on the Belah Railway, and were employed in its defence, and two days later information was received that the 75th Division would concentrate at an early date in the Deir-el-Belah Area, and orders were eventually received to be in readiness to move on the 18th August.

The Battalion was relieved on the 17th August of all Rafa duties and G.H.Q. defences, by the 1st Garrison Battalion Devonshire Regiment, and on the 18th proceeded to Khan Yunis Area. This march (at the beginning of which the boundary between Sinai and Palestine was passed) was about eleven miles in length, and was carried out in the heat of a particularly trying day. It will be remembered by all ranks as one of their most unhappy experiences in Palestine.

The following day a new bivouac area at Sheik Shabasi was reached, and here reinforcements, numbering 1 officer (2nd Lieut. J. T. Turner) and 132 other ranks, joined the Battalion. This bivouac area bordered the sea and the troops were thus able to indulge in the luxury of sea bathing. The first bathing parade was enlivened by coming under the notice of the enemy, who opened fire at a long range with one of the naval guns, supposed to have been dismantled from the German cruiser " Goeben," and used in the defence of Gaza. The shells burst high and harmlessly, but caused sufficient discomfiture to make the parade temporarily seek cover.

And so by easy stages the Battalion, during the previous four months, had gradually passed from Egypt, through Sinai, and into Palestine, until now at last it found itself within range of enemy gun fire, and face to face with the rigours of active service conditions.

In reviewing the position on the Palestine Front at this date it will be remembered that during the early part of 1917 the Turkish Army, operating in the Sinai Peninsula, had been forced back to Gaza, where it had taken up a very strong defensive position with the sea on its right flank.

The first and second unsuccessful battles of Gaza had taken place on the 26th and 27th March, and the 17th and 19th April respectively, and now the enemy's line extended from the sea at Gaza roughly along the main Gaza-Beersheba road to Beersheba, a distance of about thirty miles, and the bivouac occupied by the Battalion at Sheik Shabasi was 500 yards from the sea, and was directly in front of the Gaza defences.

General Allenby had taken over command of the Egyptian Expeditionary Force on 28th June, and it was generally known that a third attempt to capture Gaza was imminent.

The stay at Sheik Shabasi, however, was not to be of long duration, for, on 25th August, definite instructions were received to move to an area known as Apsley House, which was reached on the following day. The area in no way complied with the residential comfort such a palatial cognomen might infer; on the contrary it was a particularly desolate and cheerless neighbourhood devoid of any amenities.

The Battalion bivouacked as best it could, making the most of what shade the wadis afforded. Meanwhile, steps were being taken to introduce the Battalion gradually into the trenches at the Sheik Abbas Area; firstly officers and N.C.O.s proceeded to the line for attachment to the Argyle and Sutherland Highlanders and the 1/5th Royal Scots Fusiliers for instructional purposes, and then later on companies followed in rotation, Nos. 1 and 2 taking the first tour of duty and followed by Nos. 3 and 4. It was during the last " shift " that the first casualties occurred. A shell pitched in a wadi, out of sight of the enemy, wherein were resting a party of men of No. 4 Company, killing two and wounding twelve. Although casualties had now to be expected, yet it was unfortunate that a chance shot should have landed in such a shell trap, from which few could hope to come out unscathed. As it was, many had narrow escapes, one man having his coat, which he was using as a pillow, blown to pieces, whereas he himself was untouched. That was on the 3rd September, and the next day No. 3 Company also lost one killed and one wounded.

Training and instruction were proceeded with until the 10th, and on that day an intimation was received that the 75th Division would relieve the 52nd Division in the front line on the night of the 12/13th, and that the 233rd Brigade would relieve a part of the 155th Brigade in the Apex Sector, the 1/5th Somerset Light Infantry being detailed to take over Apex Right and Abbas Redoubt.

Consequently the Battalion left Apsley House on the 12th and marched to the trenches. The peculiar formation of the country in the Apex Sector made it possible to march right up to the front line without at any time coming under observation of the enemy, except by aeroplanes. Excellent cover was afforded by the deep wadis, and the trenches followed the line of the high ground, known as the Abbas Ridge, which bordered the wadis. From the front line trenches the ground fell away towards the enemy and formed a valley between the two lines—a distance varying from 1,200 yards to 2,000 yards.

The relief was complete before midnight, and the Companies had taken up position as follows:

No. 1 Company on Right with one Platoon as garrison of the Abbas Redoubt; No. 2 Company on Left; No. 3 Company in Centre; No. 4 Company in Reserve.

The extent of frontage held by the Battalion was approximately 2,000 yards. From now on the Battalion settled down to the routine of trench warfare. One day was very much the same as another. For an hour before dawn the Battalion would " stand to." Enemy bombardment was to be expected in the morning, as the sun, being behind the Turkish lines, was favourable to them for good observation. The reverse conditions favoured the British gunners who lost no opportunity for retaliation in the afternoon. A favourite mark was a derelict tank which had been put out of action during a previous attack on the defences of Gaza, and had fallen into the hands of the Turks. The enemy, in derision, had painted the Star and Crescent of Turkey on its shell torn side, and around they had dug a network of trenches which was known as Tank Redoubt. So conspicuous a target naturally attracted much fire.

But it was at night that the real work for the Infantry commenced, and here the subaltern officer came into his own. Patrol duties began soon after dark. The size of the patrol depended upon the nature of the work to be performed, either a reconnaissance of some portion of No-Man's-Land, or to discover if a certain wadi was occupied at night by the enemy, or merely to keep a look-out for hostile patrols. This last contingency was a constant factor in patrol work, as was only to be expected when operating in so large an area as lay between the two lines. A normal patrol would consist of 2 officers, or an officer and a senior N.C.O., and about 20 men. Badges of rank were removed and all papers and maps, etc., left behind—obvious precautions. Also rubber shoes were worn.

The utmost care was essential to ensure the success of the patrol, and with constant practice and experience the Battalion quickly became very efficient at this type of work. A complete understanding was established between leaders and men, so that parties moved in order and in silence, and were ever alert to respond immediately to the signalled command.

The fact that the allotted tasks were always carried out satisfactorily, without any casualties, speaks well for the work of the patrols, and of their leaders on whom the responsibility rested.

It must be remembered that owing to shortage of subaltern officers, each patrol leader would be out on duty every other night. On one memorable occasion—on the night of 20th-21st September—a particularly strong patrol was sent out on a special reconnaissance to see if a certain enemy outpost was occupied at night. Something evidently occurred to arouse the enemy's suspicions, and he opened a heavy and haphazard rifle fire, which was promptly and vigorously returned by the neighbouring Battalion on the left of the 1/5th Somersets. The cause of this sudden and unexpected outburst from both sides was never discovered, but the patrol remained still until the firing subsided and happily suffered no casualties, although well within the two zones of fire. As soon as the alarm had finally died down, the patrol pushed forward, completed the reconnaissance, and returned intact.

Towards the end of September the work of the patrols had one main object in view, for an order had been received from Brigade H.Q. that the 1/5th Somerset Light Infantry were to organize and carry out a raid on an enemy position known as the " Old British Trenches." To this end therefore patrol duties were focussed on that objective; also in order to lull enemy suspicion, and give an impression of anxiety to avoid active contact, patrols were ordered to retire immediately if observed and not to engage, unless compelled. The " Old British Trenches " consisted of a system of five lines of trenches, which had been dug by British troops during one of the previous attempts to circumvent Gaza, but were abandoned when the line fell back to its present position. These trenches lay about 200 yards in front of the enemy's line at Tank Redoubt, and were about 1,000 yards from the Battalion's front line. Previous reconnaissance had established the fact that this position was occupied at night. The Brigade order was to the effect that the Garrison was to be killed or captured, enemy arms, equipment, and papers collected, and prisoners obtained for identification.

On previous occasions, units occupying this part of the line had made unsuccessful attempts to raid the position, and it was considered a compliment to the Battalion to be allotted an objective that as yet had proved impregnable. Preparation for the raid was enthusiastically carried out. A model of the " Old British Trenches " obtained with the help of aeroplane photographs, had been picked out on a site behind the lines, and the details of the raid were there carefully rehearsed so that everyone engaged in the operations was thoroughly acquainted with the part he had to play.

The orders issued by Battalion Headquarters were to the effect that the Raid would be led by Capt. E. S. Goodland, M.C.:

The Assaulting Party would consist of

6 officers; 8 Assaulting sections each of 10 other ranks; 2 parties of Moppers-up, each of 6 other ranks; 4 stretchers and 8 stretcher bearers.

The Support would be under the command of Lieut. H. L. Milsom, and would consist of:

2 officers; 6 sections each of 10 other ranks; 4 signallers; 4 stretchers and 8 stretcher bearers.

The Assaulting Party and Support would leave the trenches via a gap cut in the wire, at zero − 1 hour, and proceed to the point of deployment (about 900 yards distant), where they would remain until zero, when the Assaulting Party would advance and rush the " Old British Trenches," each section having its own objective.

The object of the Raid having been carried out the signal for withdrawal (a low G on the Bugle) would be given. Until the withdrawal of the Assaulting Party the Support would use the bayonet only to keep off enemy patrols.

On the night of 6th-7th October all was in readiness at the appointed hour. Z-1 was 7.30 p.m. Two silent patrols were sent out—one by the 2/4th Hants for the left flank, and one by the 3/3rd Gurkha Rifles for the right flank. The Gurkha silent patrol was to follow after the Assaulting Party and Support Party, but owing to a slight delay in finding the gap in the wire, the Gurkhas passed across the front of the Assaulting Party. Positions were speedily readjusted, and in dead silence and grim determination the Somerset men marched stealthily towards the objective. This was to be a silent raid, unannounced by any preliminary bombardment or barrage. The guns were all in readiness behind, but their part in the display was reserved for a more subtle "coup" later on. Surprise was the essential factor, and nerves were tense lest any untoward incident should occur to give the show away. The anxieties of those taking part were in no way lessened by a break in the telephone wire, but the severed ends were soon found and the signallers speedily repaired the damage, and everything went according to plan.

Having reached the point of deployment the Supports halted and the Assaulting Party proceeded alone towards their objective. The intervening distance was quickly covered and a few shots coming from enemy posted in pits slightly in front of the "Old British Trenches," told that the approach had been discovered. Thereupon the assaulting sections advanced at the double and in a moment were among the enemy. The surprise had been so complete that little resistance was offered; every Turk who could do so fled, hotly pursued by the raiders, and very few got away. Of a garrison of perhaps thirty, at least twenty were bayoneted and killed. The survivors reaching their main line at Tank Redoubt evidently spread panic and alarm, and gave the impression that an attack in force was being launched on the Redoubt. Reinforcements were rushed into the trenches around the Redoubt, the shouting of orders and loud cries of fear were plainly heard, the Turk, as is his wont, crying upon Allah to protect him. The object of the raid being gained, Capt. Goodland ordered the signal for the withdrawal and fell back upon the Supporting Party. An orderly retirement of Assaulting Party, silent patrols, and finally Supporting Party then ensued. Precautions having been taken to tie tags of white tape, at intervals, on to the telephone wire, the way back to the trenches was easily found, only a few hostile shots being fired from an outlying enemy patrol, which had remained concealed in one of the wadis on the flank.

Whilst the withdrawal was in progress the signal to the guns had been given, and with a sudden crash the barrage opened up on the already crowded trenches at Tank Redoubt, with what result can only be imagined. But there can be no doubt that the enemy had a most uncomfortable time that night.

Once back behind the wire the raiders had time to count the cost, which slight though it was, was bad enough. The casualties numbered only one killed and two wounded, but it was Sergeant Gardiner who had fallen. He had been killed by a bayonet wound through the chest, whilst leading his section in the attack. A regular soldier who had been with the Regiment many years and had already been recommended for a commission, he could ill be spared. The other casualties were only slight wounds.

The enemy retaliated with a heavy bombardment, but too late to do any damage, as by that time the raiders were back under cover in dug-outs.

However, the 1/5th Somerset Light Infantry had every reason to be proud of the success they had achieved and of the congratulations which were immediately received from the Brigade, Divisional, and Corps Commanders, and even the G.O.C. in C., E.E.F. himself.

The day after the raid orders were received that the Battalion would be relieved by the 123rd Outrams Rifles, of the 234th Infantry Brigade, and on the night of the 8th-9th would return to the Apsley House Area.

The relief was completed at 5 a.m. on the 8th, and the Battalion remained in reserve until the 14th, when it relieved the 5th Argyle and Sutherland Highlanders in the Edinburgh Subsector of the Sheik Abbas Sector.

The routine in this part of the line—known as Lees Hill—was much the same as at the Apex. The enemy trenches on Outpost Hill, opposite Lees Hill, were only a few hundred yards away. The entire British trench system was exposed to the enemy observation posts on Ali El Muntar—a steep hill to the top of which Samson was supposed to have carried the gates of Gaza. Patrols were as usual; one difficult reconnaissance was successfully carried out by 2nd Lieut. A. M. Foster, to discover if certain trenches in No-Man's-Land were occupied by the enemy.

On the 16th a Company of the 1/4th Wilts (which Battalion had but recently arrived in Palestine), was attached by platoons to the 1/5th Somerset Light Infantry for instruction. The remaining Companies in turn were likewise initiated into the line until, on the 26th, the entire Battalion was able to relieve the 1/5th Somerset Light Infantry.

Meanwhile, certain changes had taken place in connection with Battalion Headquarters. Lieut.-Colonel Cooke-Hurle had been admitted to hospital in Cairo on the 19th. Majors E. B. Kite and D. S. Watson, having both proceeded home on leave, the command now devolved upon Major F. D. Urwick.

Capt. F. H. F. Calway had also relinquished his post as Adjutant, which he had so ably filled since October 1914, in order to take up a Staff appointment. In his place, Capt. E. S. Goodland succeeded to the Adjutancy. Capt. Goodland had already seen considerable service in Mesopotamia and had been awarded the Military Cross whilst serving with a Battalion of the Buffs.

The Battalion also lost Capt. J. Duke and Capt. J. H. Blake, both of whom were given Staff appointments. Lieut. R. B. Moore became Brigade Stokes Gun Officer, and 2nd Lieut. S. H. Elder also joined Brigadier-General Colston's Staff at Brigade Headquarters.

After being relieved at Lees Hill, the 1/5th Somerset Light Infantry moved, in reserve, to Queens Hill and the Slag Heap.

It was now very evident that a general offensive was about to take place, and speculation was rife as to how and when it would occur. Batteries of all calibre had been moved into position and were busy registering on their targets.

It is not within the province of this history to relate the full details of the offensive, which is a matter of public knowledge, but it will suffice to say that it became known at the time that the 52nd and 54th Divisions were to attack on the Gaza defences from the Cairo Road to the sea, the 75th Division was to hold the Sheik Abbas Sector, and the 10th, 60th, 74th, and 53rd Divisions were to attack on the Beersheba side.

Interest was intensified by the appearance of warships at sea to assist in the bombardment of Gaza; first a monitor appeared, soon to be joined by another, and later on two gunboats, two destroyers, and finally a cruiser. All made a very imposing display and added their quota to the bombardment.

On the day the preliminary bombardment commenced, the 27th October, a terrific thunderstorm broke over Gaza and the rain fell in torrents causing many dug-outs to collapse and trenches to be flooded out. The enemy, of course, suffered similar inconvenience, which was to tell severely when the state of the ground hindered his subsequent retirement.

As time went on, the bombardment grew in intensity until every portion of the enemy's defences was subjected to a systematic pounding. Special attention was paid to Turkish observation posts on Ali El Muntar, and also to the Mosque, which had been respected and spared until it became evident that its sacred precincts were being abused; a tremendous explosion resulting from a direct hit proved that the Mosque was being used as an ammunition dump. Excellent shooting was done from the monitors, who registered hits on far distant objects, such as bridges, to hinder the enemy's retirement. Retaliatory bombardment was only to be expected and frequently the Battalion's position had its share of the heavy shelling.

On Tuesday, 30th October, the capture of Beersheba was announced, and the news was received with great enthusiasm. Events now began to shape rapidly. Details were issued of an attack to be carried out by the 233rd Brigade on the night of X/X + 1. The 1/4th Wilts were to attack Outpost Hill and " in certain circumstances " (presumably the success of that operation) the 1/5th Somersets would attack Middlesex Hill and the Maze, which were on the right and rear of Outpost Hill.

Preparations for the attack were hurriedly carried out. Aeroplane photographs of Outpost and Middlesex Hills enabled a plan, on a small scale, to be picked out on the ground for all concerned to study.

Each Company had a definite objective allotted. Nos. 3 and 4 were to form the Assaulting Party, No. 2 the Reserve, and No. 1 the Carrying Party.

On the plan, each enemy trench was given a name and the objectives were: No. 4 Company, Rugby and Basingstoke trench; No. 3 Company, Aberdeen trench; No. 2 Company, Bath and Dover trench. A dump of ammunition, bombs, water, stores, etc., was formed in a wadi, known as the Donga, all ready to be carried forward by No. 1 Company after the attack had been launched.

All preparations completed, the Battalion waited in enthusiastic anticipation for the word to go. At the last moment, a draft of 65 N.C.O.s and men, all of whom had seen service in France with the Regiment, joined, and was split up amongst the various companies. During the preceding weeks many changes had taken place in officer personnel; many officers had been drawn from the Battalion for appointments to Staff posts, Schools of Instruction, Flying Corps, etc., or had proceeded on leave, or been evacuated sick. Consequently the numbers were considerably depleted, and the following remained to " go over the top " when the Battalion attacked: *Headquarters:* Major F. D. Urwick (Commanding Officer); Capt. A. O. Major (Second-in-Command); Capt. E. S. Goodland, M.C. (Adjutant); 2nd Lieut. W. G. Bradford (Intelligence Officer). *No. 1 Company:* 2nd Lieut. G. P. Clarke, 2nd Lieut. W. A. Hannaford, 2nd Lieut. W. Young; *No. 2 Company:* Lieut. H. L. Milsom, 2nd Lieut. C. G. Ames; *No. 3 Company:* Capt. A. S. Timms, 2nd Lieut. N. Whitley, 2nd Lieut. H. W. Elliott, 2nd Lieut. J. T. Turner; *No. 4 Company:* Capt. G. Banes-Walker, 2nd Lieut. A. Foster; Lieut. T. Moore (Transport Officer), Lieut. T. Bond (Quartermaster), Capt. E. W. Witney, R.A.M.C. (Medical Officer), Capt. E. T. Leslie (C.F.) (Chaplain).

Regimental-Sergeant-Major W. H. G. Young had recently received his commission and had been appointed to No. 1 Company. His place was taken by Company-Sergeant-Major Davis who was also granted a commission later on. Regimental-Quartermaster-Sergeant F. Stoodley ultimately was appointed Transport Officer when that post became vacant. Special mention is here made of these three senior members who had had many years service with the Battalion. They had all done splendid work, both in India and Palestine, and it was only fitting that their services should be recognized by their promotion at a time when the Battalion was being called upon to show its mettle.

Friday, 2nd November, was the day of X, and on the left—from the Cairo Road to the sea—the 52nd and 54th Divisions attacked and made excellent progress. The moment for the attack on Middlesex Hill was eagerly awaited, but to everyone's disappointment, a postponement was announced. On each of the three succeeding days, similar orders to " stand fast " were issued; the order as to whether the attack was to come off or otherwise was conveyed by means of code words, very appropriately chosen, thus " Blankets " meant " stand fast " and " Rum," " attack."

At last on the 6th orders were received that the attack would take place, the object being to pin the enemy as much as possible to the Gaza Sector, and prevent him sending troops elsewhere. Outpost Hill, Middlesex Hill, and the Maze, were to be captured and consolidated. Nos. 2, 3, and 4 Companies were to move independently to the Donga, reaching the assembly point at stated times, *i.e.*, Nos. 3 and 4 at 9.30 p.m., and No. 2 at 10 p.m. Bombs were then to be drawn and a tot of rum issued to each man. Zero hour was 11.30 p.m. and the attacking companies were to time their advance so as to strike the south part of Middlesex Hill at Zero, plus 24 minutes (11.54 p.m.).

At the appointed hour the companies assembled in the Donga Wadi, and all was in readiness for the attack, with the exception of No. 3 Company, which had been led astray by their guide and had failed to find the position of assembly. To take the place of the missing company, No 2 Company moved up from its position in reserve, and the advance held on unchecked. At zero hour, 11.30 p.m., the barrage opened with a deafening crash and by the glare of the bursting shells the enemy's wire stakes could be clearly seen. To the observer who had often scanned the dense network of wire during the days prior to the attack, it seemed impossible that such a formidable and elaborate obstacle could ever be removed. But on arrival at the enemy's line of defence, hardly a strand of wire could be found intact; the entire mass had been practically obliterated by the deadly and accurate bombardment to which it had now been subjected.

The position was stormed with ease, as the Turks had already started their retreat and left their line thinly defended. As the barrage lifted, the infantry pressed on, the men of Somerset and Wiltshire shoulder to shoulder, and, having safely reached their objectives, they consolidated the position.

The cost to the Battalion, in numbers, had been slight, the casualties being one officer and two other ranks wounded; though the loss of 2nd Lieut. C. G.

Ames, through wounds, left Lieut. H. L. Milsom, from now on, to continue the command of No. 2 Company single-handed.

Just before dawn patrols were sent forward to reconnoitre the Labyrinth and Green Hill, and as day was breaking the Battalion followed and occupied these positions without opposition. It was now clear that Gaza had fallen at last. British aeroplanes flew low and fired Verey lights as they passed over the lines occupied by the infantry, evidently indicating the extent of the advance. Ali El Muntar, that conspicuous feature which commanded a view of the whole of Gaza and surrounding country, was similarly explored by a forward patrol—as also was the town of Gaza itself. But there was little or no sign of the enemy as yet. That he had evacuated his positions hurriedly was evident by the state of the trenches and the vast quantities of ammunition, bombs, etc., left behind. But his presence on the right flank continued to be felt; shelling from that quarter commenced early in the day and continued fairly heavily throughout the morning.

At about mid-day the Battalion had occupied Fryer Hill, at the farther side of Gaza, and Nos. 3 and 4 Companies found and engaged the retiring enemy at long range. Artillery fire from the right flank in the direction of Tank Redoubt continued to give much trouble. Fortunately, the Somerset men were in extended order and well placed, but the 1/4th Wilts coming up on the left in mass formation attracted the attention of the enemy's heavy guns, and came under severe shell fire which caused many casualties.

Before attacking Gaza the infantry had been ordered to wear triangles of bright tin on the back (attached to the haversack) so that the progress of the advance could be noted by the gunners behind, and barrage fire adjusted accordingly. It is highly probable that this precaution (as far as the 233rd Brigade was concerned) only served to attract the attention of the enemy artillery on the right flank, for he opened fire with heavy guns, whose flashes could plainly be seen, and inflicted much damage—the bombardment lasting several hours. The British guns had been outdistanced by the rapidity of the advance and were not up far enough to retaliate. The Battalion's casualties on Fryer Hill were comparatively slight—owing to the advantage taken of the cover afforded—being 14 other ranks wounded.

That night the Battalion spent on Fryer Hill in the Turkish trenches, which were in a sad condition. The heavy storm of 27th October had done much damage and the trenches, especially the communication trenches, had crumbled badly.

Next day, 8th November, no move was made from Fryer Hill. The Divisions on the left could be seen advancing and the enemy was still on the run. A particularly violent explosion on the right front indicated that he had blown up an ammunition dump.

On the 10th the 233rd Brigade assembled and marched a distance of 14 miles to Ejje, where it bivouacked after a very hot and dusty march, made more irksome owing to the lack of water. The advance was continued on the following day, and the line of march was bestrewn with stores and ammunition abandoned by the enemy, none of whom, however, were encountered. The Battalion passed through Julis and reached the village of Es Suafir esh Sherkiye at nightfall, relieving the 1/5th Devons and taking over their Outpost line. Heavy rain fell during the night.

A reconnaissance forward of Sherkiye established the fact that large bodies of enemy were located near the villages of Tel El Turmus and El Kustineh. The Battalion advanced to a ridge south of these two villages, dug in, and remained in the position for the night, prepared for any contingency.

The night passed without incident, and at dawn 2nd Lieut. N. Whitley was sent out with a patrol to reconnoitre in the direction of Tel El Turmus. The patrol came under machine gun fire, but was able to report that the enemy had retired from the village. Meanwhile, preparations were carried out for the 233rd Infantry Brigade to attack and capture the two villages of Tel El Turmus and El Kustineh, and finally the further objective of El Mesmiyeh.

Battalion orders issued by Major F. D. Urwick were to the effect that No. 1 and No. 4 Companies were to attack first, followed by No. 3 and No. 2 Companies. No. 4 Company's right was to include the village of Tel El Turmus, and No. 1 Company's left to rest on the right edge of El Kustineh (which village the 1/4th Wilts Regiment were to attack). When these points had been reached, No. 3 and No. 2 Companies were to pass through No. 1 and No. 4 Companies and attack the village of El Mesmiyeh, the ultimate objective.

The first phase of the attack, *i.e.*, the taking of the two villages, passed off according to plan with only a moderate amount of shelling, and the change over of formation was effected before advancing to the second phase, which was the assault of Mesmiyeh. But at this stage it was clear that trouble was threatened from the right flank, from which quarter artillery fire had been opened, and was now augmented by heavy machine gun fire, on the troops issuing from Tel El Turmus. On observing this, Major F. D. Urwick sent a message to Brigadier-General Colston asking permission to leave one Company in that village to protect the right rear during the further advance on Mesmiyeh, as he was by then fully aware of the exposed right flank and the possibility of the Turks re-occupying the village after the attacking troops had left it. However, the order came back that he was to push on to Mesmiyeh with the entire Battalion, Turks on the right or not. Subsequent events proved how well this order was carried out.

The second phase of the attack then commenced. No. 2 Company now joined up with No. 3 Company who had already passed El Kustineh, and both advanced to the assault of Mesmiyeh, with No. 1 Company in support and No. 4 Company in reserve.

No sooner did the leading lines appear on the sky-line as they topped the ridge about 1,200 yards from the objective, than a perfect storm of heavy shell fire was let loose upon them. This was at about 10.15 a.m. But in spite of the continuous deluge of shells of all kinds, and the rain of machine gun fire through which the Battalion had to pass, the lines never wavered for one second. It was here that the splendid discipline of a well-trained Battalion told, and the work of many years of patient training rewarded. This advance of the 1/5th Somerset Light Infantry with an exposed flank and enfilade fire over a distance of some 1,200 yards, disproved all that had been previously written on the attack, as perfect direction was maintained throughout this trying ordeal. The advance was carried out without a halt except at about 500 yards from the objective, where the old Turkish railway to Gaza crossed the front of the attack, and some platoons halted to reorganize under the embankment. But only for a few moments; finding that cleverly placed machine guns searched the reverse of this embankment from the right, they at once continued their advance. At this point several Lewis guns were ordered to the right to try and keep down the enemy machine-gun fire, and the officer commanding sent the fighting portion of Battalion H.Q. under the Second-in-Command, to support these guns.

By 11 a.m. the village, surrounded by cactus hedges which formed a natural and formidable obstacle, had been rushed and captured, and the third phase, the consolidation of the position thus won, commenced. Although the village itself had fallen, the enemy continued to give serious trouble, and cleverly concealed snipers behind the cactus hedges and outlying buildings caused many casualties; the shelling was unabated. The enemy made one determined effort to retake the village from the exposed flank, but this counter attack was beaten off by well directed Lewis gun and rifle fire, and Mesmiyeh remained firmly in the hands of the West Countrymen.

In the afternoon, at 3.45 p.m., the 1/5th Somerset Light Infantry and the 1/4th Wilts were ordered to attack and occupy the Ridge about 1,000 yards north of Mesmiyeh. Accordingly No. 1 and No. 3 Companies were lent to the 1/4th

Wilts and the attack, commanded by Lieut.-Colonel Armstrong of that Battalion, was carried out with great gallantry and success. The enemy was routed out of his position and fled, leaving three machine guns in the hands of the Somersets, and a number of prisoners. Meanwhile the right flank was still held by No. 2 and No. 4 Companies. The arrival of the 3/3rd Gurkhas relieved the tension on the line, which had been weakened by the withdrawal of the two Companies to assist the 1/4th Wilts.

At nightfall the positions won had been consolidated, and so ended a day of which the Battalion may ever be proud. The 1/5th Somerset Light Infantry had fought splendidly on this 13th November 1917, and had thoroughly deserved the compliments later bestowed. The Battalion gained many honours for the distinguished part it played that day, and it was only fitting that the Commanding Officer, Major F. D. Urwick, should subsequently be awarded the D.S.O. for his conspicuous gallantry and able leadership in this brilliant action.

Considering the nature of the engagement and the terrific fire to which the Battalion had been subjected, the casualties were not heavy. This was due to the steadiness of the troops when advancing in extended order and the skill in making use of cover—all the result of patient and careful training. But the Battalion suffered the loss of 2nd Lieut. H. W. Elliott and 5 other ranks killed. 2nd Lieut. Elliott had served in the South African War and had seen much service. 2nd Lieut. J. T. Turner and 2nd Lieut. W. H. G. Young were wounded, but both remained on duty. 41 other ranks were wounded.

On the following day the Battalion moved two miles beyond Mesmiyeh and took up position facing east, where it remained until the 16th November, when a march was made to a position 1,000 yards north of Kezazeh, near the Junction Station, which had recently fallen with much booty and valuable rolling-stock into the hands of the 234th Infantry Brigade.

It was believed at the time that a lengthy stay would be made at Kezazeh. Everything was quiet and the time was spent in consolidating the position and getting up supplies. But on the 18th orders were received to be ready to move at short notice.

At dawn on 19th November the Battalion marched to the Brigade rendezvous on the Jerusalem Road, north of Junction Station, and the entire 233rd Brigade moved through Amwas and Latron. The 234th Brigade ahead evidently encountered some opposition, as later in the day the advance began to slow down.

The country had now undergone a complete change compared with that through which the victorious army had advanced since Gaza fell. Instead of open, cultivated plains, it now became very precipitous and rocky. The advance had reached the foot of the Judaean Hills. Climatic conditions, too, became more trying to the troops, clad as they were only in thin khaki drill.

At dusk the column had reached the entrance to the Pass of Beth-Horon and the Battalion started to climb the Pass, for the possession of which the 234th Brigade ahead was fighting. Such heights as had been taken were picketed; but before proceeding very far, a sudden outburst of machine gun fire checked the advance, and at every twist of the tortuous and difficult road (which had also been mined and destroyed in places) a similar welcome was given by the enemy, who evidently still held the heights in force.

Consequently as it was impossible to clear the Pass in darkness, it was decided to withdraw the advancing column and bivouac at the Latron end of the Pass. The road being congested with animals and transport of all kinds, this withdrawal was carried out with great difficulty. To add to the general discomfort it rained heavily during the night.

As soon as daylight appeared the Battalion again essayed the Pass and encountered no serious opposition. At the top, however, the 232nd Brigade had been held up and to relieve matters, the 1/5th Somerset Light Infantry and 1/4th Wilts were lent to that Brigade, commanded by Brig.-General Huddlestone, and were ordered to attack and capture Kuryet El Enab. It was absolutely essential to take the village that night, so that the troops could get water, of which there was a serious shortage.

Orders were quickly given and without more ado the attack was launched. No. 2 and No. 4 Companies led, with No. 3 Company in support and No. 1 Company in reserve. It had been the intention to bombard the objective for half an hour previous to attacking, but a providential and heavy shower of rain descended like a blanket over the hill-top, and under cover of the mist the lines immediately advanced. Armoured cars on the roadway gave covering fire. In spite of very heavy rifle and machine-gun fire from the Turks defending Kuryet El Enab, the lines advanced with great coolness and gallantry, and without a halt captured the position, sending the enemy headlong in swift retreat. On hearing that the objective had been captured the G.O.C. of the attacking Brigade sent a message to the Division that " The Somerset Light Infantry have taken Enab. Am moving my Brigade into the village." The casualties were slight, 2 killed and 9 wounded.

This brilliant action brought the 1/5th Somerset Light Infantry into much prominence. On Saturday, 24th November 1917, the War Office issued a Bulletin from which the following is an extract: " General Allenby further reports that the successful action of 19th November, when the enemy were driven from the defile west of Kuryet El Enab, was due to the gallantry of Somerset, Wiltshire, and Gurkha regiments."

On hearing the news the G.O.C. in Chief in India, General Monro, wrote a personal letter to the O.C. of the 1/5th Somerset Light Infantry warmly congratulating him and saying he felt sure the Battalion mentioned must be the same splendid Battalion he had known in India.

The night that followed was exceedingly wet and it was under wretched conditions that the Battalion bivouacked on the outskirts of the village. No sooner had dawn appeared than the enemy announced his presence with a salvo of gun-fire, and continued shelling heavily for two hours. Fortunately the Battalion's position was screened from the enemy's view, but other units were not so lucky and, congested as they were, suffered heavy casualties. So crowded were men, animals, transport, etc., that not a shell fell without terrible effect. One shell alone caused 30 casualties and another landed amidst a group of officers of the 3/3rd Gurkhas, wounding the C.O. and many others.

At 10.30 a.m. the 233rd Brigade marched via the old Roman road, which leaves the Jerusalem road on that side of Enab and runs north. The old Roman road was but a rocky track which necessitated moving in single file. Desultory and inaccurate shelling greeted the Battalion at the outset, but soon ceased. As the track reached its highest point a splendid view of Jerusalem was seen, the Holy City being about eight miles on the right front.

By the afternoon a point south of the village of Biddu was reached and the Battalion bivouacked for the night with No. 2 Company forming outposts on the right flank. Meanwhile the 234th Brigade ahead had attacked and captured Nebi Samwil.

It was now evident that the enemy was concentrating on the defence of Jerusalem, and was occupying very strong positions in force, with many guns.

Shortly after dawn the outposts were withdrawn and, with scant time to snatch a hasty breakfast, the Battalion was again on the move. Orders had been given for the 1/5th Somerset Light Infantry with the 1/4th Wilts Regiment, to advance and capture the villages of El Jib and Bir Nebala, with a final objective, the village of Kutundia. So the Battalion set out with its sister Battalion of the neighbouring county, both under command of the Senior Commanding Officer, Lieut.-Colonel Armstrong of the 1/4th Wilts. A squadron of Hyderabad Lancers and a section of Machine Guns accompanied the expedition. Two Companies of the 1/5th Somersets led the advance under the command of Capt. A. O. Major and, with the Cavalry, formed the vanguard. Leaving Nebi Samwil on the right the attacking force advanced in a northerly direction, presumably to avoid coming into view of the enemy and being shelled. Lieut.-Colonel Armstrong himself went with and directed the advanced guard, and Major Urwick led the two remaining Companies of the 1/5th Somerset Light Infantry and the 1/4th Wilts Regiment. Marching in this precipitous country was very difficult and unfortunately direction was lost. So instead of turning east towards El Jib the O.C. the attacking force continued the advance northwards, mistaking the only village visible, Beitunia (which lay some five miles away), for El Jib.

The enemy was holding a high hill in the path of the advance and the leading Companies soon came under fire. The remaining two Companies of the Battalion were then thrown into the attack, but Battalion Headquarters were left with the 1/4th Wilts. On reaching a valley which lay between the Battalion and the enemy, temporary cover was afforded by this " dead " ground, and the Somersets now started a slow and laborious climb up the precipitous side of the hill. Tired out as they were—for there had been little rest the last four days—the men found it extremely difficult to negotiate the huge boulders which encumbered the hillside. But they stuck to their task grimly and even succeeded in dislodging the Turks from their forward positions on the crest of the hill.

The advantages, however, all lay with the enemy, who was cleverly and strongly placed on a further ridge, and snipers took terrible toll as the exhausted troops clambered into view over the boulders. The O.C. Attacking Force, displaying great courage, was himself in the forefront of the fight, doing his utmost to stimulate the attackers to still greater efforts; but Companies had got hopelessly intermixed, as could only be expected in an advance over such difficult ground. Men were dead beat and, perhaps, a little discouraged by the extremely difficult conditions under which they had to fight. Also the knowledge that they were temporarily divorced from the direct control of their own headquarters did not tend to raise their spirits. No covering fire was possible, though Lewis gunners strove gallantly to support the attack. Of artillery there was none to reply to the heavy shelling the Somersets had to endure.

Yet, in spite of all this, the survivors clung bravely and desperately to the ground they had gained, keeping the enemy's line constantly under fire and awaiting the necessary reinforcements before the last final rush could be made.

But at what a cost! Capt. G. Banes-Walker had been shot dead whilst leading his men in a gallant attempt to dislodge the enemy. A very popular, keen, and efficient officer, his death was a sad blow to the Battalion. 2nd Lieuts. W. G. Bradford, N. Whitley, and J. T. Turner, had all been wounded. Altogether the Somerset casualties numbered 10 killed, 26 wounded, and 2 missing.

Lieut.-Colonel Armstrong threw his own Battalion into the fight, but the Wiltshiremen met with no better success and lost heavily, as they made brave but futile attempts to reach and support their Somersetshire comrades.

Meanwhile, communication had been established with Brigade Headquarters, and orders were given to hang on till nightfall and then retire on the village of Beit Izza.

As soon as it was dark therefore, the withdrawal of the Battalion commenced, covered by the 1/4th Wilts. The dead were collected and buried, and the wounded picked up and carried down the hill. All day long the stretcher-bearers had worked heroically, endeavouring to succour the wounded, but their task was impossible, and many a man suffered terribly through lying out all day with his wounds untended. Now the stretcher-bearers had the greatest difficulty in carrying the wounded down the rocky and precipitous hillside. Slowly and painfully the descent was made.

At the foot of the hill the survivors of the Battalion assembled and reorganized. As the line of retirement on Beit Izza ran along a valley on the right in the enemy's direction before turning off to Beit Izza, and as a body of Turks had been seen advancing at dusk for a counter-attack, Major Urwick took the precaution of sending three Companies ahead under Capt. Goodland, followed by the wounded. Last of all, he himself marched with No. 2 Company who had bayonets fixed and orders to charge if attacked.

Slowly and laboriously the procession wended its way to Beit Izza, which was safely reached without further incident, and the Battalion there went into bivouac for the night.

At dawn of Friday, 23rd November, the news came that El Jib had yet to be taken, and preparations to launch the attack were immediately made. El Jib is a natural stronghold, standing on a high hill and guarded by steep rocky terraces. The approach is through a valley 600-700 yards wide, with the ridge of Nebi Samwil on the right and high ground and terraces on the left leading from Beit Izza.

The Battalion was now sadly depleted in strength, and so heavy had been the casualties that one Company, No. 3, had no officers at all. So Company-Sergeant-Major Windows assumed command of No. 3 Company, and for his gallantry that day was subsequently decorated.

At 8 o'clock the Battalion reached the entrance to the valley leading to El Jib and deployed into extended order for the attack, No. 1 and No. 3 Companies leading, No. 4 in support, and No. 2 in reserve. Orders were to advance under the protection of the slopes of Nebi Samwil—the Mosque thereon being in the hands of the 3/3rd Gurkhas—and to scale the rocky terraces at the right end of the valley, then to swing left towards the village itself. The 2/3rd Gurkhas were to follow and push on to Bir Nebala when El Jib had fallen.

As soon as the attack had been launched and the extended lines emerged from the entrance to the valley, the enemy artillery put down a terrific barrage of high explosive shells and shrapnel. Through this inferno of shell-fire the attackers advanced with the greatest courage, keeping perfect formation as if on parade. But worse was to come, for on passing through the artillery barrage the lines came under a veritable hail of bullets from enemy machine guns in front, the northern slopes of Nebi Samwil on the right, and the high ground on the left. This devastating enfilade fire from all sides wrought terrible havoc and the lines seemed to melt away.

It had been supposed that the whole of the Nebi Samwil ridge had been captured, but, apparently, the attack had only reached as far as the Mosque, beyond which the enemy was still strongly placed and able to bring an unexpected enfilade fire from that quarter. Also it must be remembered that no British artillery had succeeded, as yet, in getting up far enough to support the attacks on the enemy positions near Jerusalem. Hence the only supporting fire for the assault on El Jib came from machine guns and a Mountain Battery.

All four Companies and any of Battalion Headquarters who could be spared had long been thrown into the attack, and, in spite of heavy casualties and almost insurmountable obstacles, the survivors pressed on without a check and actually reached the terraces of the village. Unfortunately, these terraces were so high and steep that it was almost impossible to climb them, yet there were some who were not to be denied. It is to be recorded in these annals with real pride that three Lewis gun sections succeeded, with great difficulty and bravery, in scaling these terraces. They were all either killed or taken prisoners and their guns lost, but their deed remains an heroic example for all time. When, many weeks afterwards, El Jib ultimately fell, the identity discs of twenty-seven very gallant Somersets, who had climbed the terraces, were recovered.

By this time every officer was either killed or wounded. To assist the Battalion the 1/5th Devons were thrown into the attack on the left. The 2/3rd

Gurkhas too pressed forward. But these efforts were brought to nought, so fierce was the enemy's fire, and the attack was at a standstill. Owing to the accuracy of hostile fire, no runner succeeded in getting back to Battalion Headquarters or in reaching the attacking line, so communication was impossible. There was nothing for it, therefore, but to lie still and take advantage of what cover was available.

At nightfall the Battalion was ordered to withdraw. A sad and difficult task then commenced. The enemy debouched from his stronghold and from his advantageous position on the higher terraces threw bombs on the retiring Somersets. The dead and wounded he robbed of clothing. Painfully and slowly the wounded, who could stand, limped back; and the few gallant survivors, who had come through unharmed, laboriously carried their more seriously wounded comrades to the shelter of the bivouac area.

Time there was now to reckon the cost, which, as has already been indicated, was very heavy. Capt. A. O. Major had been wounded by a rifle bullet early in the advance and was finally killed outright by a shell. He was a fine Christian gentleman and a brave soldier. 2nd Lieut. W. A. Hannaford, too, was missing and known to have been killed; he had only joined the Battalion in August. Of the remaining officers, Lieut. H. L. Milsom, 2nd Lieuts. G. P. Clarke and A. M. Foster were wounded. All told, 10 had been killed and 141 wounded; in addition, there were 32 missing.

The strength of the Battalion had been reduced by half in these last two days' fighting, and of the officers there remained only the Commanding Officer and the Adjutant.

Though unsuccessful in achieving the impossible, the 1/5th Somerset Light Infantry had lost nothing in reputation, but considerably added to their laurels in these two tragic days of hopeless endeavour.

During 24th November the remnants of the Battalion rested in the shelter of the bivouac area under Beit Izza, but unfortunately, there were further casualties during the morning, for nine other ranks were wounded by shell fire, and several animals were killed. On this same day a complete Brigade of the 52nd Division passed through the Battalion bivouac and attempted the assault of El Jib, but their advance was checked soon after it was launched, and the same devastating fire of the Turkish defenders which the 1/5th Somersets, the day before, had faced with such fearlessness and gallantry, prevented this Brigade making any headway, and the project was then definitely abandoned until such time as the artillery could be brought up to give the attacking infantry adequate support.

That night the 1/5th Somersets were ordered back to Enab, and the march was carried out with great difficulty. The men were still thoroughly exhausted and boots and clothing were now worn out; eventually, however, the Battalion occupied a bivouac area under the Ridge at Enab which it had captured with so much dash and distinction on 19th November, and here it remained and rested during the 25th.

The following day the Brigade moved back to Junction Station—thence to Ramleh and Ludd, and finally, on 30th November, reached Jimzu, where a part of the line, held by the 54th Division, was taken over.

During the first few days of December the Battalion remained in Brigade Reserve in an olive orchard at Jimzu, and the work of reorganizing the companies proceeded. The men were now issued with serge clothing and overcoats which added very much to their comfort, and on the 5th December, Lieut.-Colonel E. F. Cooke-Hurle rejoined from hospital and once again took over the command of the Battalion. The weather during these days was particularly severe, heavy rain fell and the nights were bitterly cold. In Palestine during December, January, and February, the rainy season is at its height, and the rain pours down ruthlessly and unceasingly for two or three days at a time, but in the intervals the climate is ideal with hot sunny days, but much of the country, devoid of metalled roads, becomes a heavy and congealed mass of mud, and makes all movement of transport and troops extremely difficult.

On the 9th December the Battalion moved to Ramleh and bivouacked on very wet and muddy ground, but there was general rejoicing when it became known that on this day Jerusalem had been completely surrounded by our troops and surrendered by the enemy. It was impossible, however, to conceal a little disappointment, because the Battalion had been denied the glory of participation in the final capture of the Holy City, but there will always remain the satisfaction of having played a considerable part during the November operations, in forcing a passage through the narrow defiles of the Judaean Hills, in securing positions of immense importance in the immediate neighbourhood of Jerusalem and in paving the way to final victory.

The following day the Battalion moved into a clean and sandy area at Surafend, and the Brigade passed into Corps Reserve. Lieut.-Colonel E. F. Cooke-Hurle temporarily assumed command of the Brigade, and Major F. D. Urwick again took over the command of the 1/5th Battalion Somerset Light Infantry. The Battalion remained in Corps Reserve at Surafend until 18th December, when it moved to Hadithe into Divisional Reserve, and bivouacked in a stony wadi, where large working parties were supplied every day for road making under the instruction of the Royal Engineers.

Christmas Day, 1917, was spent at Hadithe in atrocious weather, but the heavy rain was unable to damp the spirits of the officers and men, who thoroughly enjoyed the special rations that were obtained from Cairo, and the contents of the parcels in the Christmas post. Since the arrival of the Battalion in Palestine and during the whole time the unit was on active service, consignments of gifts arrived with wonderful regularity from the Somerset Voluntary Help Association. These extra comforts—clothing and games—were greatly appreciated by the men, and helped very materially to alleviate the discomforts of a strenuous campaign.

On 26th December the Battalion moved into the front line south of Beit Nebala, and relieved the 2/4th Battalion Somerset Light Infantry, and on 31st December Lieut.-Colonel E. F. Cooke-Hurle returned from Brigade Headquarters to take command of the Battalion. During the month the following awards were announced for conspicuous bravery during the November operations: *Distinguished Conduct Medal:* C.S.M. Windows; *Military Medal:* Sergeant J. Peppin, Private W. Cridland, Private W. H. Rowsell, Private B. Greedy, Private J. Hooper; *Military Cross:* Capt. A. S. Timms, 2nd Lieut. J. T. Turner. Regimental-Sergeant-Major Davis and Regimental-Quartermaster-Sergeant Stoodley were granted well deserved commissioned rank.

During December many officers and men had reached the Battalion as reinforcements, some fresh from England, others rejoined from hospital. These were a very welcome addition to the depleted ranks of the companies, and on 31st December the ration strength of the Battalion was 25 officers and 518 other ranks.

The first few weeks of 1918 passed by without any action of special importance; the Battalion was frequently on the move, sometimes in the front line at Beit Nebala, then in Divisional Reserve at Hadithe and then into Corps Reserve at Ludd. At this time when the available tracks and improvised roads had become quagmires of mud, owing to the rains, there was much transport difficulty. The camel had become immobile and it was often necessary to use teams of eight mules to draw the transport carts, which were frequently above their axles in the sticky mud. It was only through the untiring efforts of 2nd Lieut. F. Stoodley, who had been recently appointed Transport Officer, that all difficulties were surmounted and the Battalion was never short of rations and water. In the front line the time was chiefly devoted to patrols and to practising rifle and Lewis gun firing in No-Man's-Land, for the British and Turkish lines were some distance apart, and when in reserve, there were always large working parties needed for road making. Several matters of domestic interest may, however, be recorded. Early in January Lieut.-Colonel E. F. Cooke-Hurle again left temporarily to command the Brigade, and shortly afterwards proceeded on leave to England. On 13th January Major D. S. Watson returned from home leave, but almost immediately left for Cairo for a Senior Officers' Course, and it was about this time that official information was received that Major F. D. Urwick had been awarded the D.S.O. for distinguished service in the Mesmiyeh operations on 13th November.

During February notification was received that the 233rd Brigade would shortly be inspected by H.R.H. The Duke of Connaught, who had recently arrived in Palestine, and the 1/5th Somersets were given the distinction of supplying the Guard of Honour for the occasion, and during the time the Battalion was in reserve there was much preparation and training for this, while many large parties were needed for road making, etc.

With the advent of March orders were issued for the further advance of the first line, and in order to take part in this, the Battalion left its pleasant camp at Ludd, and moved to Hadithe and from thence to Kibbiah. The first stages of the advance of the 75th Division had been in every way successful, and the 1/5th Somerset Light Infantry being in reserve the whole time, were not actively engaged with the enemy, but on 18th March the Battalion relieved the 1/5th Devons in the front line at Khurbet-el-Emir, with headquarters in the Wadi Ballut. Meanwhile the Duke of Connaught had arrived at Ramleh, and on 16th March there was a parade, partly spoilt by the extremely wet weather, at which His Royal Highness presented decorations to the following officers, and men of the 1/5th Battalion Somerset Light Infantry: *Distinguished Service Order:* Major F. D. Urwick; *Military Cross:* Capt. A. S. Timms, Capt. E. S. Goodland; *Distinguished Conduct Medal:* R.S.M. Windows; *Military Medal and Bar:* Sergeant G. Collard; *Military Medal:* Private H. Rowsell, Private E. Petvin, Private W. Cridland, Private B. Greedy.

The Guard of Honour, consisting of Capt. E. S. Goodland, Lieut. T. Moore, and Lieut. C. G. Ames and 100 other ranks, was on parade and was inspected by His Royal Highness, who congratulated the Officer Commanding on its smartness. Subsequently the following copy of 21st Army Corps letter to Headquarters 75th Division was received:

" H.R.H. The Duke of Connaught has been pleased to express his satisfaction with the smartness, turn-out, and precision of the fine Guard of Honour mounted by the 1/5th Bn. Somerset Light Infantry on the 16th March. The Corps Commander desires that the Commanding Officer of the Battalion may be informed." The Major-General commanding the 75th Division and the G.O.C. 233rd Brigade added their appreciation of the smartness of the Guard on parade.

During March Lieut.-Colonel E. F. Cooke-Hurle returned from home leave to resume command of the Battalion, and Major D. S. Watson rejoined from the Senior Officers' Course to become second-in-command. On the 15th notification was received that Lieut. G. P. Clarke had been awarded the Military Cross, for conspicuous gallantry displayed in the November operations.

Towards the end of the month there was a further advance of the front line to Wadi Lehman, and during this operation, in which three men were wounded, the enemy artillery was very active and it was evident that the Turks would oppose in strength any further advance by the British Force. The Battalion was destined very shortly to be at grips once more with the enemy, and after some months of comparative inactivity, there was much excitement and preparation when it was known early in April that the 75th Division would make a further advance and secure the line Berukin—Sheik Subih—Arara—Rafat, and that the capture of the two latter positions had been allotted to the 1/5th Battalion Somerset Light Infantry. On 6th April Battalion Operation Orders were issued by the Commanding Officer, Lieut.-Colonel E. F. Cooke-Hurle, an extract of which is as follows:

" To-morrow, Jellalabad Day, the Battalion will advance to the line Rafat—Arara, 1st Phase, No. 4 Company (Capt. T. Moore) and No. 2 Company (Major F. D. Urwick) will assemble at 0415 hours and advance to the Northern slopes of Wadi Lehman. At 0510 hours after the artillery and machine gun barrage has lifted, No. 4 Company will rush the village of Rafat and seize it.

" 2nd Phase. No. 1 Company (Lieut. C. G. Ames) at 0700 hours will rendezvous in Wadi Lehman and when ordered will advance on the S.E. peak of Arara. No. 2 Company will deploy in the Wadi Lehman in readiness to advance on the S.W. peak of Arara. No. 3 Company (Lieut. J. Stuart) will be in reserve."

Before daylight came the 1st Phase of the operations had been carried out with the greatest success, for No. 4 Company, advancing in the darkness up the stony northern slopes of the Wadi Lehman, and following closely behind the artillery and machine gun barrage, had seized and secured with great dash the little village of Rafat, standing on the Ridge above. Three prisoners were captured and four dead Turks were found in the village, and twenty of the enemy, mostly Germans, were killed as the Garrison retreated from their positions. At dawn a heavy Turkish bombardment was opened on the village and the Wadi

Lehman, and during the day and the following night the enemy counter-attacked and made several determined efforts to recapture the ground they had lost, but these were all successfully beaten off. Owing to the troops on the right of the Battalion being unable to secure all their objectives, there was now a considerable delay, and the 2nd Phase of the attack was postponed until the following morning. During the day's fighting the casualties in the Battalion had been 1 officer (Lieut. D. Maloney) and 4 other ranks killed, and 3 officers and 32 other ranks wounded.

On the following day, 8th April, at dawn the 2nd Phase of the advance was ordered to begin after a preliminary bombardment, and the objective of the 1/5th Battalion Somerset Light Infantry was Arara. Arara was a rugged hill, devoid of all vegetation, and strewn with boulders and stones; it stands out a landmark for miles around, and was a position of great natural strength. Stretching from the village of Rafat to this Hill was a prominent ridge fashioned principally from solid rock and interspersed with enormous boulders, which became very formidable obstacles in the advance, but afforded excellent natural cover. It was against this ridge and the hill of Arara that No. 1 Company on the right and No. 3 Company on the left, advanced as soon as daylight came, No. 2 Company being in reserve and No. 4 Company still holding Rafat. At the outset things went very well indeed, for No. 3 Company, pressing on over the difficult ground with great gallantry and in the face of heavy rifle and machine-gun fire, seized the Ridge and in the determined enemy counter-attack which followed, 2nd Lieut. H. Franks of No. 3 Company distinguished himself by working a hostile machine gun which had just been captured, with deadly effect, and helping very largely in beating off the advancing Germans and Turks. The assaulting companies (Nos. 1 and 2) then proceeded to attack Arara, but almost immediately No. 3 Company were exposed to heavy and accurate fire from three machine guns firing from the N.W. peak of the hill, and were pinned down to the boulders on the Ridge. Meanwhile No. 1 Company had made good progress, and although exposed to heavy machine-gun fire, had succeeded in pressing on to within 100 yards of the summit of Arara. Here, however, they came under severe enfilade machine-gun fire from enemy positions on their right flank, which had not been captured by the other units in the Division according to plan, and it was with the greatest difficulty that the Battalion was able to hold on to the ground it had won. Until the attack on the right developed, nothing further could be done, and No. 3 Company, consolidating their position on the Ridge during the day in spite of heavy enemy artillery and trench mortar fire, managed to deal successfully with several attempts the Turks and Germans made to recapture their lost positions. When darkness came two platoons of No. 2 Company were sent to strengthen No. 1 Company on the slopes of Arara, and another heroic effort was made to rush the Hill, but by this time the enemy had been strongly reinforced and had at least four machine guns in position. Moreover, the enemy's enfilade fire on the right flank was still very deadly, and although the men in the leading attacking lines reached the summit, it was found to be untenable and the project was abandoned, No. 1 Company being withdrawn to Wadi Lehman before dawn, and No. 3 Company still being left in possession of the Ridge.

Until 19th April the Battalion hung on grimly to the positions they had won, but the situation was an extremely anxious one, for Rafat and the Ridge became a very acute salient in the line of the Division, and throughout these days there was continual shelling by artillery and particularly by trench mortars, and being overlooked from Arara with its battery of machine guns the men on the Ridge were unable to move during daylight hours and were pinned down cramped and uncomfortable behind the boulders.

The Battalion obtained a well earned rest when, on 19th April, it was relieved by the 1/4th Duke of Cornwall's Light Infantry, and passed into Divisional Reserve, and the following day the Commanding Officer received a letter from General Colston, G.O.C. 233rd Brigade, in which he said: " Will you please convey to all ranks my admiration of the dash and endurance shown by the Unit under your command during the recent most trying operations. I can best describe the work of the Battalion as worthy of the finest traditions of the famous 13th Light Infantry."

During the operations from 10th to 19th April the Battalion had lost in casualties 1 officer (2nd Lieut. E. W. Gould) and 8 other ranks killed, 4 officers and 70 other ranks wounded, and 7 other ranks missing, believed killed.

There now followed several months during which no operations on a grand scale were attempted on the Palestine front. In France, during March, the long gathering storm had broken and the great German offensive had swept across the British positions on both sides of the Somme and the effect of this serious reverse was felt in Palestine. General Allenby had been ordered to release immediately two at least of his British Divisions for service in France, and to mix his remaining White formations with Indian troops. Coinciding with this weakening of the British Force was the obvious fact, portrayed in the recent operations, that the Turks had been considerably heartened by the inclusion in their front lines of the German battalions, who had recently arrived with their own machine guns, trench mortars, and artillery, and that they were now a much more organized, better equipped, and more vigorous enemy than at any time during the campaign. For the time being, therefore, it seemed unlikely that the Battalion would be called upon for any further advance and attacking, and orders for a Defence Scheme were issued in which second and third lines of defences were included. The Battalion was frequently in and out of the front line positions, and these consisted chiefly of filthy fly and flea-infested villages perched on the summits of hills such as El Kefr, Deir Ballut, and Berukin. During these periods there was always severe enemy shelling to be contended with, always night patrols and the distribution of propaganda in No-Man's-Land, and always the inevitable casualties.

On 30th April, during a particularly heavy bombardment of El Kefr, 3 other ranks were killed and 3 wounded, and while in occupation of front line positions during May, June, and July, there were 4 other ranks killed, and 2 officers and 22 men wounded. Moreover, the strength of the Battalion was continually sapped by admissions to hospital with fever, dysentery, and other diseases consequent upon a long campaign in the East, and during August, 13 officers and 136 other ranks were evacuated sick. The periods spent out of the front positions were used up in improving second and third line defences, in supplying large working parties for road making, and in disinfecting and washing, for now at last there was ample water. Some of the bivouacs were pleasantly situated in shady wadis under olive and fig trees; opportunities were given for officers and men to visit Jerusalem, and parties were sent to the Rest Camp at El Arish.

The story of these few months would not be complete without recording the following immediate awards dated 6th May, for conspicuous bravery during the Rafat operations: *Military Cross:* 2nd Lieut. H. Franks; *Distinguished Conduct Medal:* Sergeant B. Crocker; *Military Medal:* Lance-Corporal J. Welch, Lance-Corporal P. Hughes, Lance-Corporal E. Hookings, and news was received in June, with the greatest pleasure by all ranks in the Battalion, that the Commanding Officer, Lieut.-Colonel E. F. Cooke-Hurle had been awarded the D.S.O. in the King's Birthday Gazette.

And so the summer of 1918 passed. Towards the end of August, when the numbers of the Battalion had been made up to Establishment by the inclusion of 4 officers and 223 other ranks of the 2/4th Dorset Regiment, which unit had recently been disbanded, secret information was received that shortly the offensive would once again be taken on the Palestine front, and that the Battalion would be called upon to play its part in the scheme of operations. At the time this information was received the Battalion was occupying the front line positions of Berukin, Toogood Hill, and Tinhat, but it was soon apparent that its final destination for the coming attack was somewhere on the Plain of Sharon, and consequently on the night of 4th-5th September the Battalion was relieved of all front line duties in the Hills by the 2/154th Infantry, and moved back to the Rentis Area, when for a few days special training in open warfare was carried out.

On 12th September there was a further move under cover of darkness to a bivouac area near Deir Tureif—thus bringing the Battalion a little nearer the Plains, and on the night of 16th-17th September, the Mulebbis area was reached. This came under the heading of a " concealed bivouac "; the men were hidden in orange groves and no lights or fires were allowed, each man being issued with a ration of solidified alcohol for individual cooking purposes, and all unnecessary movement was forbidden. Thus the Battalion was taking part in an immense and secret concentration of troops in the Plain, and information was now received that the day of the great attack was to be 19th September and zero hour 0430. The task allotted to the 75th Division was the important one of capturing the strong enemy Tabsor defences, and then to push through as quickly as possible beyond Et Tireh and the Tireh Defences, and for these operations the 233rd Brigade was placed in reserve. Two companies, however, of the Battalion (Nos. 2 and 3 Companies) under Major D. S. Watson, were to be attached to the 234th Brigade for the first phase of the operations, and it was the duty of these companies at zero hour to attack and seize the Turkish most advanced outposts, so that the Infantry of the units following should not be checked at the outset of the fighting. There was, therefore, much movement of troops throughout the night of 17th-18th September, and the Battalion, marching from the Mulebbis Area, took over the whole of the front line occupied by the units of the 3rd and 7th Divisions, and during the night of the 18th-19th Major Watson's two companies were deployed in position in No-Man's-Land in front of the line held by the 234th Brigade.

Zero hour came at last and there burst forth the terrific roar of the British bombardment, over a thousand shells a minute being hurled into the enemy's lines. The two companies under Major Watson's command immediately went forward to the attack, and by 0445 hours had successfully captured the Turkish advanced posts allotted to them, and two prisoners and one machine gun were taken. The Turkish first and second line trenches were strewn with dead and wounded, for nothing could have withstood the tremendous onslaught of the

British guns; the task of the Infantry was therefore made comparatively easy, and everywhere along the enemy positions from Three Bushes Hill to the sea the enemy's line was pierced by the assaulting troops. Having lost 2 other ranks killed and 5 other ranks wounded in these early operations, the two companies under Major Watson's command ultimately rejoined the Battalion and the 233rd Brigade then reformed and followed the general advance in reserve. The whole of the objectives allotted to the 75th Division were captured with wonderful rapidity and success, and only at the Tireh Defences was there a temporary check, but this enemy opposition was quickly dispersed and the 233rd Brigade was therefore not called upon for any further serious action.

With the taking of Tireh the Division had completed its task, and the 1/5th Battalion Somerset Light Infantry rested close to the village of Miskeh, and later in the day moved to a bivouac area east of this village. The Division had been squeezed out of the general advance and came into Corps Reserve. It was a great disappointment to be denied the further fruits of victory, but it was left to the mounted troops, the armoured cars, and the most mobile guns, and the Royal Air Force to continue the pursuit of the now thoroughly demoralized and disorganized Turkish Armies. The story of this pursuit, the rout, and almost complete annihilation of the enemy is now a matter of common knowledge, and the 1/5th Somersets have the satisfaction of having taken some small part in what proved to be one of the most spectacular and most crushing victories on the field of battle military history has ever known.

After a few days' rest at Miskeh, the Battalion moved to the Kalkilieh Area and there, during the remaining days of September and throughout October, the men were chiefly occupied in salvage work and in road making, and it was on the 31st of October that Battalion Headquarters received the following wire: "An Armistice has been concluded with Turkey by terms of which hostilities between the Allies and Turkey cease at 1200 to-day."

During the first week of November the 233rd Brigade moved back to Hadithe and the Battalion found itself once more in a familiar bivouac ground. It was here that on 11th November the great news that an Armistice with Germany had been signed was received. There was intense joy and satisfaction amongst the officers and men, and the day was given up to general rejoicing and celebrations.

But beneath the excitement and gratification of complete victory there was the feeling of profound relief in the minds of all ranks that the Great War was over, and that after more than four years' exile in the East they would soon be turning their faces towards Home and the fertile vales and hills of Somerset once again.

CHAPTER V

ARMISTICE TO RETURN OF CADRE TO TAUNTON IN JANUARY 1920

THE War History of many Battalions practically concludes with the Armistice and cessation of hostilities, but the 1/5th Battalion Somerset Light Infantry was destined to see more than a year's further service in the East ere the Cadre returned to Taunton early in 1920. Many of these months were taken up with the routine and the ordinary garrison duties of a unit of the Army of Occupation, but Egypt at this time was extremely unsettled, and there were often important duties to be carried out by the Battalion—notably the part it played in restoring order in Upper Egypt after the serious riots in March 1919—and this History would be incomplete without some record of these months of further service.

It will be remembered that when news of the Armistice came, the Battalion was at Hadithe busily employed on road making and training, and now large parties of officers and men were allowed to proceed on short leave to Cairo and Jerusalem, and many were also detailed to attend various courses of instruction at Zeitoun and El Arish. It was not until 6th December that another move was made, and then the Battalion marched to Ludd and with the other units of the 233rd Brigade proceeded by train to Kantara, and here demobilization was soon to begin in earnest. It is of interest to place on record the following letter received on 11th December from the Officer Commanding the Depot, Somerset Light Infantry, Taunton:

To the Officer Commanding,
  1/5th Somerset Light Infantry.
SIR,
  I am requested to convey to you the following resolution passed at the meeting of the Taunton Town Council on 12th November 1918 to which I have duly replied.

"That the Town Council of Taunton at their first meeting after the signing of the Armistice desire, on behalf of the inhabitants of the County Town, to express to the officers and men of all Somerset units, their unbounded admiration for the valour they have displayed in upholding, during the Great War, the glorious traditions of Somerset soldiers, and their deep gratitude for the great part which they have played in the accomplishment of victory for the cause of Right."

Yours faithfully,
(*Signed*) L. JONES MORTIMER,
Major.
Commanding Depot Somerset Light Infantry.

The time at Kantara passed pleasantly enough, for all ranks were enjoying the comfort of a standing camp with ample rations and water, and the opportunities for sport and recreation this enormous Base provided, and soon Christmas Day arrived. The festive season was celebrated with much enthusiasm and enjoyment, reminiscent of the days in India. Each Company had been provided with a large mess tent, to which the Colonel made a tour of visits, and there was an abundant supply of turkeys—the frozen variety—and plum puddings. It was a very different Christmas Day from that spent in the rain soaked bivouac at Hadithe a year ago. During December Capt. and Quartermaster R. Stone was posted to the Battalion to replace Capt. and Quartermaster T. Bond, and he remained with the unit until the Cadre returned to England. Capt. Bond, after many years' devoted service, had been sent home sick soon after the Armistice, and his departure was regretted by all ranks.

The New Year came with demobilization proceeding apace, and on 7th January the Battalion moved across the Canal and went into another standing camp beside its blue waters on the Egyptian side, and although large parties of four and five hundred men were required daily for different duties, there was ample time for football, fishing, and bathing, and the constant stream of shipping passing up and down the Canal was a source of perpetual interest. A Divisional Education School was now opened and classes were formed in a great diversity of subjects, by which the men were able to renew their school days, and a limited number of skilled and unskilled tradesmen were given practical instruction by being attached to the various workshops at Kantara. During January the following further awards were announced: *Military Cross:* 2nd Lieut. S. H. Knight; *Distinguished Conduct Medal:* Sergeant T. Field, Corporal G. Knight.

On 17th February an event of the utmost importance and interest occurred in the Battalion's history, for on this day the Commanding Officer, Lieut.-

Colonel E. F. Cooke-Hurle, D.S.O., left the camp by the waters of the Canal and departed to England with orders to report to the War Office. Every officer and man turned out to bid him farewell, and although most members of the band had already been demobilized, yet three or four were found who made a brave show of the Regimental March. It was with a real sense of personal loss that the Battalion parted with the Colonel, for all ranks from the humblest private upwards had learnt to regard him as a friend for whom they had the greatest affection, and to whose high character and reputation for the strictest fairness they could look at all times with confidence and constant inspiration. Whether in barracks, or in camp, or in the field, his chief concern was the welfare, comfort, and safety of his officers and men. To him the Battalion owed its training, its efficiency, and its discipline, and the laurels it had won on the field of battle were largely due to his influence and guidance. On relinquishing command Lieut.-Colonel Cooke-Hurle issued the following farewell letter to all ranks:

On leaving the Battalion after more than 6 years as Commanding Officer, I wish to place on record my appreciation of the services rendered by all ranks during my tenure of command. The loyalty and support given me by Officers, Warrant Officers, N.C.O.s and men have made my duties easy, and I am deeply grateful for your trust and confidence. Your devotion to duty under all circumstances has given the 1/5th Battalion Somerset Light Infantry a name that will not be forgotten. Whether in barracks—on service—in attack—or during the long trying days and nights in the front line, your spirit has always been the same. You have done your duty unhesitatingly and nobly, and I am confident that no Commanding Officer in the British Army has been better served by all ranks, from first to last, than I have.

My best wishes go with you all for health and happiness and a successful career in the future. I am proud to have commanded you.

(*Signed*) E. F. COOKE-HURLE,
Lieut.-Col. Commanding 1/5th Battalion Somerset L.I.

Major D. S. Watson, who had been awarded the Distinguished Service Order as a result of the final operations in Palestine, had already been demobilized and was on his way home, but by great good fortune, Major F. D. Urwick, D.S.O. had recently rejoined from leave to Ceylon, and was therefore able again to assume command of the Battalion. For some weeks nothing of importance occurred to disturb the routine of camp life but by the end of February, demobilization had so depleted the numbers of the Battalion that the ration strength had been reduced to only 363 men.

There was therefore every indication that very soon the 1/5th Battalion Somerset Light Infantry would be reduced to only cadre strength and would be embarking and proceeding on its journey homewards, but on 16th March all the feelings of unrest in the country, and hatred of the British, were suddenly fanned into flame and, from north to south, Egypt was shaken by the most serious Nationalist riots she had ever known; and so the Battalion, as a result of this upheaval, was delayed in the East for many months to come.

With all haste all available troops were rushed to restore order in towns and villages and to guard railways, bridges, and vital points, but everywhere the cry was "Egypt for the Egyptians," and the situation was extremely critical. No. 1 Company, consisting of 5 officers and 150 men, were despatched on 24th March to Bilbeis for guard duties in the district, in which was situated an enormous Prisoners of War Camp, and on 26th March the Headquarters of the Battalion and the remaining three companies were hurriedly despatched by rail from Kantara to Cairo and went into camp on Roda Island. Before leaving Kantara, actually at the railway station shortly before the departure of the train, the Battalion was reinforced practically up to full strength by 9 officers and 623 men from the Demobilization Camp. This large draft arrived at short notice, without nominal rolls, and comprised men from practically every unit in the E.E.F. There were representatives of the Highland Light Infantry, the Connaught Rangers, the Manchesters, the Seaforths, the Royal Irish, and many others— truly a composite Battalion. These men had been hurriedly organized on the eve of their departure for England. Their feelings of acute disappointment and annoyance may well be imagined, and it was with the greatest difficulty, naturally, that order was restored and discipline maintained under these chaotic conditions.

At Cairo it was learned that the destination of the Battalion was Upper Egypt, and 27th March was occupied in drawing and fitting summer clothing, and in hastily reorganizing companies. Throughout Upper Egypt, from Cairo to Assouan, there had been extensive damage done by the rioters during 16th, 17th, and 18th March; in many places the railway had been torn up and bridges destroyed, railway stations and the houses and bungalows of British officials had been burnt out, and the Luxor train had been attacked and British officers foully murdered by the infuriated mob. The native police had been powerless, and everywhere there had been appalling loss of life and property.

On 28th March the Headquarters of the Battalion with Major F. D. Urwick, D.S.O. in command, and No. 2 and 4 Companies, with Major Clarke, a political officer attached, left Cairo *en route* to Wasta as escort to the train detailed to repair the railway, and the following day, No. 3 Company embarked at Giza Wharf, and proceeded to Wasta by river boat. No. 1 Company was still at Bilbeis, but ultimately rejoined the Battalion at Wasta on 1st April.

For the first day or so the situation was normal and the work of repairing the railway line and bridges proceeded satisfactorily, but on the evening of 30th March the village of Shobak-el-Ghaffari, adjoining the railway, was reached, and here the train and its escort met with a hostile reception. The train halted near the village owing to a break in the line, and a small party of men, unarmed, went into Shobak-el-Ghaffari to buy butter and eggs. They had scarcely reached the outskirts of the village when they were fired on and the natives rushed at them with knives and sticks, and they had considerable difficulty in getting back to the train. A platoon was ordered out to clear the village and during the street fighting that ensued the houses and huts caught fire, and eight men of the Battalion were wounded. Five of the ringleaders, caught red-handed using firearms, were arrested and were shot at dawn the following day, while the Omda was taken to Wasta and handed over to the civil authorities.

By 3rd April the duty with the constructional train ended and the whole Battalion concentrated at Wasta, but it was soon to be separated again for more than a month, for on the 4th, Nos. 3 and 4 Companies, under Capt. W. J. F. Austin, entrained for Beni Suef, to join a column operating in that district. This column, which was under the command of Lieut.-Colonel Massey of the 29th Punjabis, became known as Massey's Column, and in the meantime, Headquarters with No. 1 Company and No. 2 Company, were ordered to prepare to move up river by steamer with the Force under General Colston's command. This latter Force embarked at Wasta on 5th April, and to the 1/5th Battalion Somerset Light Infantry was allotted the steamer S.W.8. with Major Keith as political officer. Two lighters were attached to the steamer for the accommodation of the troops, transport, and stores, and the animals proceeded in dhows towed along by a small tug.

For six days the convoy steamed up the Nile, meeting with little trouble or outward hostility from the villages along the banks and, indeed, participating in a delightfully interesting river trip only possible under ordinary peace-time conditions to people of wealth and leisure. Ultimately on 11th April Mallawi was reached and here the Battalion disembarked. This area was known as No. 3

Section and the garrison, which included a troop of the 12th Australian Light Horse and other details, came under Major Urwick's command. Owing to the prompt and adequate Military precautions taken, there was little difficulty in restoring order in the disturbed areas of Upper Egypt, and already the people of the towns and villages were continuing their peaceful occupations. The garrisons both at Mallawi and Beni Suef were chiefly occupied in guard duties and in demonstration marches and reconnaissance. Almost daily neighbouring villages were surrounded and searched for suspected persons and fire-arms, but, on the whole, little trouble was experienced. The reputation of the Battalion for dealing promptly and sternly with hostility had rapidly spread, after the affair at Shobak-el-Ghaffari, throughout the villages on both sides of the Nile, and henceforth the men of the 1/5th Somersets were treated with the greatest respect.

Towards the end of April Headquarters and No. 1 and No. 2 Companies, which had been operating in the Mallawi area, were moved by train to Beni Mazar, and finally on 8th May were despatched to Cairo, where at Polygon Camp they were joined by the two Companies which had formed part of Massey's Column at Beni Suef, and so the Battalion was once more united for a few days. With the immediate despatch, however, to the Demobilization Camp at Kantara of all the men so suddenly drafted to the Battalion for the operations in Upper Egypt, the ration strength was reduced to 22 officers and only 220 other ranks, and the 1/5th Somersets therefore became only a skeleton of its former self.

It was now confidently expected that the Battalion would be reduced to cadre strength and that its tour of duty in the East would cease, but the situation in Egypt, especially in the large and populous towns, still gave cause for much anxiety, and G.H.Q. were loath to part with British Units. Consequently there were further duties allotted to the Battalion, and on 20th May, Headquarters and No. 1 and No. 4 Companies were despatched to Suez and No. 2 and No. 3 Companies to Bilbeis.

By the beginning of June demobilization was practically completed, and the Battalion received several parties of Army of Occupation men from other units and a most welcome Draft of 181 other ranks joined from the 3rd Battalion Somerset Light Infantry, then stationed in Ireland, and in this way its strength was partially maintained.

The garrison at Bilbeis was almost entirely occupied in guard duties in connection with the Prisoners of War Camp, and remained in this Area until the final break-up of the Battalion in the following November. The detachment at Suez first of all occupied Arbain camp on the outskirts of the town, and ultimately moved on 20th June to the standing camp at Port Tewfik, close to the Canal, where there were many and varied duties to carry out. There was little opportunity either at Bilbeis or Suez for any training or concentrated work, owing to shortage of personnel, but everything possible was done to maintain the high efficiency of the Battalion, and as far as duties would permit, the men were encouraged to engage in all kinds of sport, including cricket, football, and water polo.

July came and found the Battalion both at Suez and Bilbeis, taking part on the 14th in celebrations and rejoicings arranged for the Signing of Peace with Germany, and the summer passed to autumn with the same daily round of duties and routine work, and during this time Major F. D. Urwick, D.S.O., having commanded the Battalion for the prescribed period, obtained his promotion to Lieut.-Colonel, and Capt. E. S. Goodland, M.C. his promotion to Major as Second-in-Command, and Lieut. S. W. Mason was appointed Adjutant.

At last, on 22nd November, the Battalion, having disposed of its officers and men to other units of the Army of Occupation, and scattered its specialists to formations throughout the Forces in Egypt and Palestine, was reduced to a cadre strength of 3 officers and 43 other ranks. It was not, however, until 11th December that the cadre of the Battalion left Port Tewfik for the Rest Camp at Port Said, there to await orders for embarkation. The 1/5th Somerset Light Infantry, during its tour of duty at Suez and Port Tewfik, had become very popular with other units in the Area, which included a Royal Air Force Squadron and an important Transit Camp, had made many friends among the British and French colonies and remained on good terms with the local inhabitants, and the send-off the cadre was given was a memorable one. The cadre was inspected by the Base Commandant, bands played, flags were flown, and the Royal Air Force provided a formation of aeroplanes as escort to the train as far as Ismailia.

There was a further delay in the departure for home at Port Said, but eventually the cadre, which now consisted of Lieut.-Colonel F. D. Urwick, D.S.O., Major E. S. Goodland, M.C., Lieut. L. C. Ambrose, and 43 other ranks, proceeded to Alexandria, and sailed for England on the White Star liner " Teutonic " on Christmas Day. After calling at Malta and Gibraltar the voyage home was uneventful, except that extremely rough weather was encountered in the Bay of Biscay, and finally the troops were landed at Plymouth on Tuesday, 6th January 1920.

Thirty-six men of the 1/5th Somerset Light Infantry were ordered to proceed to Fovant for demobilization and consequently the cadre, which immediately proceeded to Taunton, consisted of only 3 officers and 7 men. Amongst the latter was the Regimental-Sergeant-Major, J. Burrows, who as a Lance-Corporal had left with the Battalion for India in 1914. The following day the cadre was given a public welcome and a civic reception at the Municipal Buildings, where they paraded with the Depot Band, and afterwards were entertained to luncheon, over which the Mayor, Alderman H. J. Van Trump, presided.

And so comes to an end the story of the 1/5th Battalion Somerset Light Infantry, and its record of service in the Great War. For more than five years the Battalion had carried out its innumerable and varied duties in the East honourably and with the greatest credit, and all ranks had proved themselves worthy of the famous Light Infantry Regiment to which they belonged. In India, in Mesopotamia, in Palestine and Egypt, there remain those officers, N.C.O.s and men of the Battalion who laid down their lives for their King and Country and for the cause of Right. To these Glorious Dead this Book of Remembrance will remain a lasting Memorial, and maybe to those who come after, to carry on the traditions of the Battalion, a constant inspiration.

HONOURS AND REWARDS

MENTION IN DESPATCHES

BLAKE, Captain A. L.
BRADFORD, Lieutenant W. G.
COOKE-HURLE, Lieutenant-Colonel E. F.
CORADINE, Lieutenant A. J. B.
GOODLAND, Captain E. S. (2)
MOORE, Captain T.
RAWLINGS, Captain G. W.
STUART, 2nd Lieutenant J.
URWICK, Major F. D.
WATSON, Major D. S.

CHAMBERLAIN, Sergeant E.
DULBOROUGH, Sergeant J.
ENO, Sergeant H.
FROST, Corporal L.
JENNINGS, Corporal A. R.
MASTERS, Corporal W. H.
MOORE, Private A. W.
PAVEY, Sergeant S. C.
PENNY, Lance-Corporal A.
TAYLOR, Private J.

REWARDS

O.B.E.

BLAKE, Captain A. L.

M.B.E.

PAVEY, Lieutenant G. P.
STOODLEY, 2nd Lieutenant F.

L

D.S.O.

COOKE-HURLE, Lieutenant-Colonel E. F.
URWICK, Major F. D.
WATSON, Major D. S.

M.C.

CLARKE, Lieutenant G. P.
FRANKS, 2nd Lieutenant H.
GOODLAND, Lieutenant E. S.
KNIGHT, 2nd Lieutenant S. H.
TIMMS, Captain A. S.
TURNER, 2nd Lieutenant J. T.

D.C.M.

CROCKER, Sergeant B.
ENO, Sergeant H.
FIELD, Sergeant T.
GREGORY, Corporal F.
KNIGHT, Corporal G. T.
TRENCHARD, Sergeant S.
VENN, Corporal W. J. D.
WILTSHIRE, Sergeant W.
WINDOWS, Company-Sergeant-Major W. C.

M.M.

CADDY, Private A.
COLLARD, Sergeant G.
CRIDLAND, Private W.
GREEDY, Private B.
HAYSHAM, Private E.
HOOKINGS, Lance-Corporal E.
HOOPER, Private J.
JENNINGS, Corporal A. R.
PEPPIN, Sergeant J. B.
PETVIN, Private E. V.
RAFFILL, Private J. W.

HONOURS AND REWARDS

Rowsell, Private H. J.
Welch, Lance-Corporal J.

Bar to M.M.
Collard, Sergeant G., M.M.
Jennings, Sergeant A. R., M.M.

FOREIGN DECORATIONS

EGYPT

Order of the Nile, 4th Class
Calway, Captain F. H. F.
Duke, Captain J.

FRANCE

Croix de Guerre
Goodland, Captain E. S., M.C.

Medaille d'Honneur avec Glaives " en Vermeil "
Burrows, Regimental-Sergeant-Major J.

ITALY

Order of the Crown of Italy (Chevalier)
Duke, Captain J.

ROUMANIA

Order of the Crown of Roumania

Officer

Cooke-Hurle, Lieutenant-Colonel E. F., D.S.O.

MESOPOTAMIA

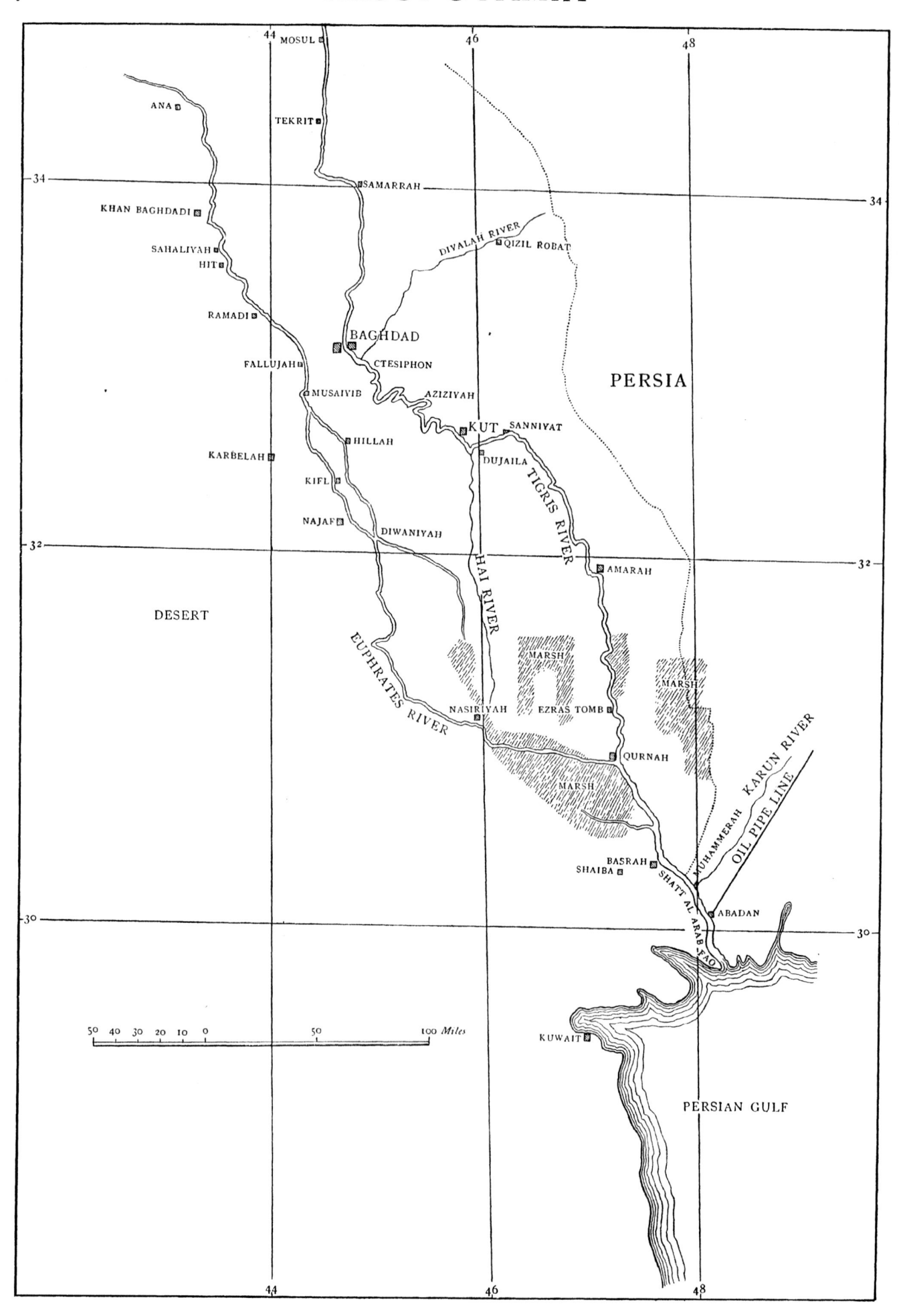

PALESTINE

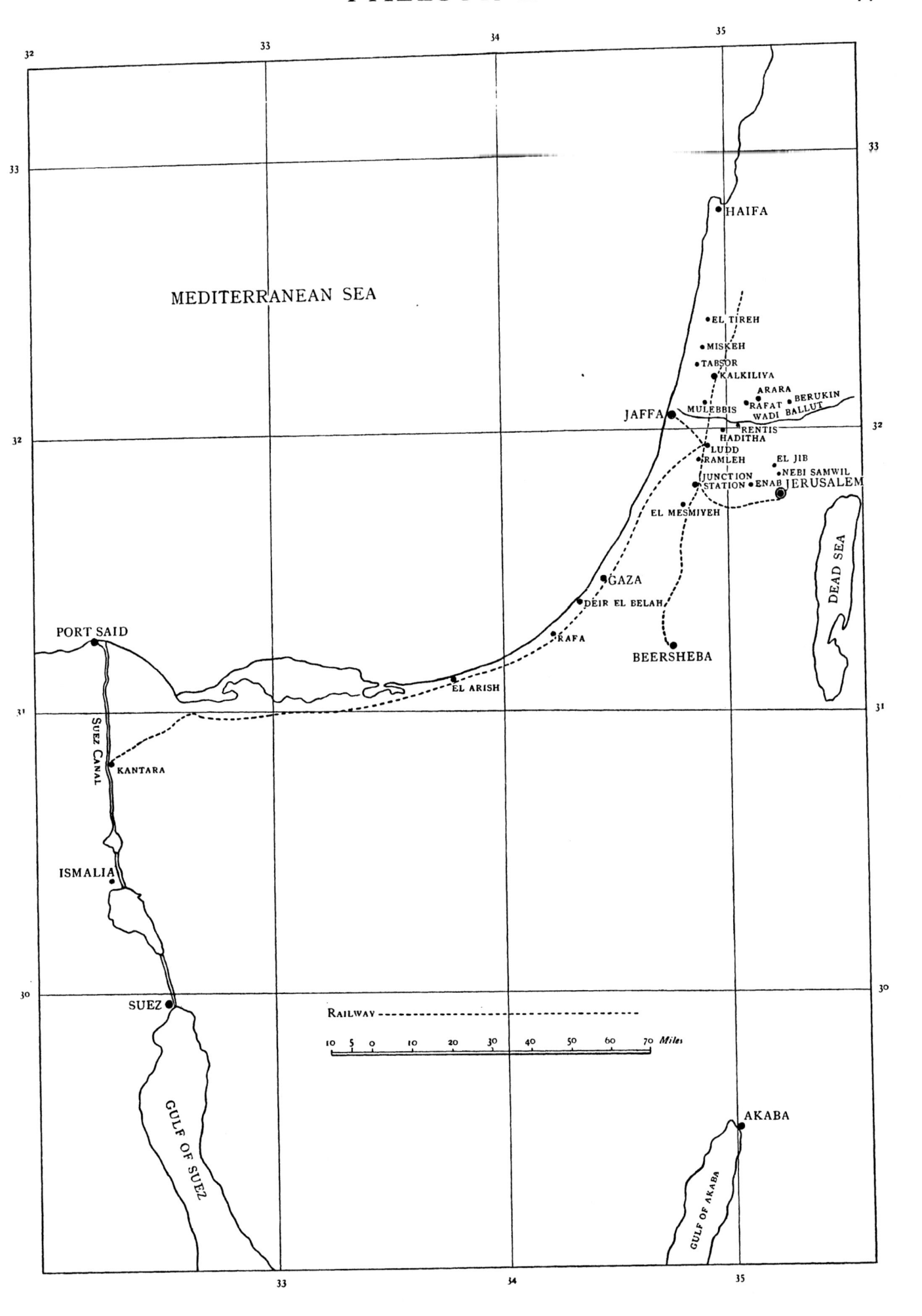

THE HISTORY

OF THE

2/5TH BATTALION (PRINCE ALBERT'S)
SOMERSET LIGHT INFANTRY

WRITTEN AND COMPILED BY

MAJOR C. H. GOODLAND, CAPTAIN T. M. PULMAN,
CAPTAIN SIR J. S. P. MELLOR, BT., CAPTAIN
A. H. ARMSTRONG, CAPTAIN W. E. HUNT,
AND LIEUT. J. BELL

1930

FOREWORD

"They also serve who only stand and wait."

IN a recent article by that eminent military historian, The Hon. Sir John Fortescue, based on a newly discovered daily order book of the Richmond (Yorks) Militia when embodied and quartered in Newcastle in that year of Victories, 1759, he says: " While its pages were slowly filling up, news had come in that Knox had stormed Masulipatam, that Barrington had conquered Guadeloupe, that Ferdinand of Brunswick had beaten Contades at Minden, that Wolfe had beaten Montcalm at Quebec, and that Hawke had vanquished Conflans in Quiberon Bay; and little though they suspected it, these Militia men had borne their share in these victories by liberating the Regular Forces for service overseas."

That is the opinion of the greatest living British Military historian writing in the cold light of history 170 years after the event, and long after the glamour of the victories themselves had passed away.

So also from 1914 till the end of the Great War those Territorial Battalions who had not the fortune to take an actual part in the fighting line did their share by setting free the army from the duty of maintaining peace and order throughout His Majesty's vast Empire, and so contributed to every victory won.

As regards those Battalions which went to Burma, all the Line Battalions liberated by them formed part of the immortal 29th Division whose services at the Dardanelles will never be forgotten while military history is read; the 2/5th Somerset Light Infantry may well be proud of the fact that but for them, and the other Territorial Battalions in Burma, that magnificent Division could not have been formed.

The 2/5th Somerset Light Infantry arrived in Burma at a critical moment. A rising had taken place of some of the hill tribes in the north; serious indiscipline had just occurred in Rangoon, and worse was to follow in Singapore within a week or two. With their arrival we were enabled to concentrate so formidable a force at Myitkyina in the extreme north of Burma that the revolted tribes hastened to submit; and at the same time we were able to send a Battalion to the assistance of the hard pressed government in Singapore.

From the moment of their arrival the 2/5th Somerset Light Infantry, which was composed of men of fine physique, set energetically to work to perfect themselves in all branches of military training, spurred on, no doubt, by the hope that they in their turn would eventually go to the fighting line; and, although that hope never materialized, they soon made themselves fit in all respects to take their place with credit and distinction on any battle-front. Meanwhile they did their part in the War by guarding great camps of Turkish prisoners, and by the strength and confidence they contributed to the Government of India through those anxious years, until the crowning victory, made possible by them, at length arrived.

I am glad this record of their services has been compiled, and only hope that their fellow-countrymen in Somerset will realize the important services rendered by them.

H. L. Pritt.

Major-General,
Commanding Burma Division 1914-18.

December 1929.

CHAPTER I

FORMATION

ARMY Order 399 of September 1914, which authorized the formation of a Home Service Unit for each Battalion of the Territorial Force accepted for Imperial Service, brought the 2/5th Battalion into being.

The men were ready. They had responded in overwhelming numbers to the Recruiting Appeal of the Company Commanders of the 5th Battalion, who, at the end of August, had been sent by Lieut.-Colonel E. F. Cooke-Hurle into their Home Districts in anticipation of this development. They were attested at Taunton, having first signed the Imperial Service obligation, sent on to Durrington Camp, Salisbury Plain, on 14th September, and moved to West Down South a few days later.

Here the Battalion was formed. Major J. R. Paull, T.D., and Capt. C. H. Goodland were transferred from the Parent Battalion as Commanding Officer and Adjutant respectively; to it were drafted the N.C.O.s and men who were surplus to the requirements of the Field Service Battalion.

Early in October the 2/5th Battalion, or the 5th (Reserve) Battalion, as it was then called, went into billets at Taunton.

Gradually it took shape. Officers were posted from various sources. Most of them had family associations with West Somerset, those of previous experience being Major W. H. Speke, Capt. W. Winter Goode, and Capt. C. Ward Jackson. The men were of first-rate stamp, mainly from Taunton, Bridgwater, Yeovil, Chard, Ilminster, Langport, Watchet, Minehead, Wellington, Wiveliscombe, and the surrounding villages.

For two months training went forward steadily at Taunton. At the very end of November the Battalion received orders to move to the outer defences of London, around Guildford. The baggage was on rail. The day before departure the Commanding Officer was summoned to an urgent conference at the War Office. India had called again. To their utter surprise the Units of the Second Wessex Division found they had been selected to follow their field service comrades to the East.

The Battalion at this time numbered 1,055 of all ranks—of whom 970 had volunteered for Imperial Service. Only 800 could be taken, this number being the full complement of an Indian Field Service Battalion. The men who were surplus and those medically unfit for foreign service, together with the Home Service N.C.O.s and men, were taken over by Capt. W. T. Burridge (who also had been transferred from the 5th Battalion). This nucleus was transferred to Prior Park, Bath, in February 1915, and from it was formed the 3/5th Battalion, with Major, afterwards Lieut.-Colonel H. W. H. Heathcoat-Amory as Commanding Officer. The summer of that year was spent in camp at Cheddar, and the winter in billets at Winton, Bournemouth. In the spring of 1916 the unit was moved into hutments at Hursley Park, near Winchester, and, later in the year, amalgamated with the 3/4th Battalion, with the designation 4th (Reserve) Battalion Somerset Light Infantry. It was thus a Training Unit, and provided reinforcements for the overseas Battalions throughout the War.

CHAPTER II

BURMA

THE Battalion embarked at Southampton on 12th December 1914 in the hired transport "Ionian" for Bombay, the ultimate destination being Burma.

The officers were: Lieut.-Colonel J. R. Paull, T.D. (*Commanding*); Major W. H. Speke; Capt. C. H. Goodland (*Adjutant*); Capt. W. Winter Goode; Capt. C. Ward Jackson; Lieut. T. M. Pulman; Lieut. H. H. Broadmead; Lieut. J. S. P. Mellor; Lieut. N. D. Blake; Lieut. A. H. Armstrong; Lieut. W. S. Hearn; Lieut. A. M. P. Luscombe; Lieut. J. Cook; Lieut. F. E. Spurway; 2nd Lieut. R. B. Marsh; 2nd Lieut. Hon. A. P. Acland Hood; 2nd Lieut. M. Brooks King; 2nd Lieut. R. O. Hobhouse; 2nd Lieut. C. F. B. Pearce; 2nd Lieut. G. A. G. Vallance; 2nd Lieut. D. F. Irving; 2nd Lieut. A. E. J. Gawler; 2nd Lieut. J. L. Steele; 2nd Lieut. C. N. Price; 2nd Lieut. R. C. H. Riddell; 2nd Lieut. J. Bell; 2nd Lieut. H. N. Whiting; Lieut. and Quartermaster T. H. Hood; Lieut. A. D. Fraser, R.A.M.C. (S.R.).

Christmas Day, 1914, was spent at Port Said. Here occurred the first casualty, Private E. C. Williams of Taunton. He had died at sea the previous day and his body was taken on shore and buried in the English cemetery.

Immediately on arrival at Bombay, 8th January 1915, the Battalion entrained for Calcutta, a four days' journey of much discomfort in coaches utterly unsuited for the conveyance of troops. After seven days in tents on the Maidan, around Fort William, the voyage across the Bay of Bengal was continued in a most uncomfortable hired transport, the s.s. "Thongwa." At the mouth of the Rangoon river transhipment was made into an Irrawaddy Flotilla Steamer, with its accompanying barges, and the next stage—up the Irrawaddy River—was begun.

One afternoon the steamer was made fast to a sand-bank to enable the men to get much needed exercise and a bathe in the backwater. They rejoined ship one man short—for Private Fred Board, of Dowlish Wake, had slipped off the edge of the shallows into the main stream, and was drowned.

On 1st February 1915 Headquarters, with "B" and "C" Companies, reached

Meiktila, about 80 miles south of Mandalay, and 300 miles north of Rangoon. "A" and "D" Companies, under Major W. H. Speke, were taken on to Mandalay. Here they were transhipped into a smaller river boat and reached their station, Shwebo, in the heart of the plains of Upper Burma, three or four days later.

The Battalion deserved a rest. Departure from England had been at such short notice that proper kits had not been received for issue. The voyage of well over 9,000 miles in four separate stages, in three different extemporized troopships, together with the long railway journey across India under strange climatic conditions, with unsuitable clothing and insufficient kit, under commissariat arrangements of which none of the officers had any previous experience, had been borne with much cheerfulness and fortitude, reflecting great credit on all ranks.

But it was not to be. On 16th February a most urgent telegram was received from Brigade Headquarters, Rangoon, ordering one Company from Meiktila and one Company from Shwebo to proceed thither by first train. Capt. C. Ward Jackson with "C" Company and Lieut. H. H. Broadmead with "A" Company were detailed. They found on arrival at Sale Barracks,[1] Rangoon, that they were taking the place of the 4th Battalion King's Shropshire Light Infantry, which had been despatched to Singapore at a few hours' notice to quell a disturbance that had suddenly arisen there.

Thus the duties of the British Infantry Garrison of Rangoon were added to the responsibilities of the 2/5th Battalion, and remained so for nearly a year. Major W. H. Speke was transferred from Shwebo early in March to command this detachment.

During the next five months great progress was made in the improvement of organization, and in training. Mobilization equipment and stores were collected, and the Battalion re-armed. Many officers and N.C.O.s were sent over to India for specialist courses at training centres. Machine gun and Signalling sections were formed. Bugle Major Hughes was so successful in training the Buglers that the absence of a Regimental Band was rarely noticed.

On 7th August 1915 a draft of 40 N.C.O.s and men, under the command of Lieut. J. S. P. Mellor, left Rangoon for service with the Indian Expeditionary Force D. A detailed account of the experiences of this Draft will be found in Chapter III following.

Capt. C. H. Goodland, who had been Adjutant of the Battalion since its formation, vacated this appointment on promotion at the end of August, being

---

[1] Named after Sir Robert Sale, commander of "The illustrious garrison of Jellalabad."

transferred to the command of " B " Company. Capt. T. M. Pulman succeeded him.

On 6th September a change over of Companies was made. " B " Company from Meiktila and " D " Company from Shwebo proceeded to Rangoon, whilst " C " Company returned to Shwebo and "A" Company to Meiktila. Musketry became the principal work at the up-country stations, while at Rangoon the guard and garrison duties became more arduous as the tension of internal security became more strained. So serious was the situation considered on Christmas Day that under orders of Brigade the troops at all stations were confined to barracks, and the detachment at Rangoon ate their Christmas dinner with their rifles between their knees. This discomfort, however, was lightened by the generosity of the British Residents of the city, who sent up to the barracks an abundance of Christmas fare.

With the New Year came a change. On 5th January 1916 a Territorial Garrison Battalion, the 18th London Rifle Brigade, arrived from England and relieved the Rangoon Detachment, which immediately returned to Upper Burma. A very cordial message of appreciation was published by the Brigade Commander on their departure. For eleven months two Companies of the Battalion had carried out in Rangoon the important guard and picquet duties normally distributed over double their number. Capt. W. W. Goode with " D " Company returned to Battalion Headquarters by river, escorting a large party of Turkish prisoners of war as far as the Internment Camp at Thayetmyo. No sooner, however, had this Company reached Meiktila than it was ordered back to Thayetmyo for guard duty. Here, strengthened by 50 men of " A " Company, Capt. Goode's Company remained until 17th August, when it returned to Meiktila.

Major C. H. Goodland with " B " Company left by rail for Shwebo. On arrival orders were found directing this Company to proceed immediately to Bhamo on the Irrawaddy, 1,030 miles due north from Rangoon, to take over the British Infantry Barracks, which had been unoccupied for a couple of years. This entailed a long day's march to the river at Khaukmyoung and a week's voyage up stream in the R.I.M. steamer " Bhamo."

A pleasant cold weather station Bhamo was found to be, with good training facilities. The Company soon settled down in their quarters inside the old Fort and established friendly relations with the Indian Infantry Regiment also stationed there, and the detachment of Burma Military Police. Bhamo is close to the frontier, and is the river port on which trade routes converge from the Chinese province of Yunnan, and the wild hill country of the Kachins. Its curious medley of inhabitants, Shans, Kachins, and Chinese, together with the constant stream of caravans, formed a never failing source of interest.

Major Goodland was recalled to Divisional Headquarters, Maymyo, at the end of January for training in staff duties.

On 29th February "B" Company, numbering 5 officers and 131 other ranks with elephant and mule pack transport and a large number of native followers, left Bhamo for a march through the Kachin Hills to the Chinese frontier. Major W. H. Speke was in command, and the other officers were Lieut. N. D. Blake and 2nd Lieuts. C. N. Price and J. Bell, with Captain White, R.A.M.C., in medical charge. The object of the march was to impress upon the frontier tribes, who were becoming restive, the fact that the whole British Army had not yet been exterminated.

The route lay over a range rising to a height of between 5,000 and 7,000 feet, roughly in a S.E. direction, the first objective being the important market-town of Namkham, situated in a plain in the extreme north of the Shan States, immediately adjoining the frontier of China. Namkham is six days' march from Bhamo, and the track is rough and steep, running at first through rugged mountainous country and afterwards over a fertile and thickly-populated plain on the banks of the Shweli river, which was crossed by a narrow bamboo bridge some 250 yards in length.

A great impression was made at Namkham, where the detachment, headed by four buglers, marched with fixed bayonets through the crowded bazaar, and the belief that there were no more British soldiers in existence was effectively dispelled.

The route taken now followed the course of the Namwai river, which forms the boundary between British and Chinese territory, and after a march of five days in a northerly direction the detachment reached Loije, situated upon the great trade route between Burma and Tengyueh in the Chinese province of Yunnan. It is believed that no European troops had ever been seen in this district before, and as the advance party arrived at each village it was found to be deserted, the inhabitants having fled in terror at the sight of white men. After an hour or two, however, they invariably returned and proved friendly enough, and the operations of pitching and striking camp formed a perpetual source of amazement.

From Loije the route led westward over ranges which rose to 6,000 feet, and after four marches Bhamo was reached again on 18th March. The total distance covered was nearly 200 miles, and in spite of the rough and arduous character of the country and the extremes of heat and cold which were met, the health of the detachment remained excellent throughout. The experience was a memorable one to all those who took part in it, and the political effect in the wild regions along the frontier was undoubtedly good.

"B" Company returned to Shwebo about the middle of April.

During the summer Drafts from England arrived. One Draft which sailed in the s.s. "Ceramic" had an eventful voyage and narrowly escaped disaster in the Mediterranean from an attack made upon it by an enemy submarine with shells and torpedoes. These Drafts were a welcome reinforcement; the officers rendered valuable service in many ways and several stayed with the Battalion until the end; the men were a good lot, and quickly made friends with their comrades in the Companies to which they were posted.

The health of the Battalion remained good, and continued progress was made in efficiency and preparedness for service in a theatre of war.

Late in the year, on 1st November, for internal security reasons, "A" Company was transferred to Rangoon to strengthen the garrison there, Major W. H. Speke being again sent from Shwebo to command the detachment.

The visit which His Excellency the Viceroy—Viscount Chelmsford—made to Burma in December will be remembered by many officers and men of the Battalion. Capt. W. W. Goode with "D" Company was moved to Rangoon for special duty in this connection, and returned to Headquarters after an absence of three weeks.

During the early months of 1917 the fullest opportunities were taken to make further progress in field training and musketry. Exhaustive tests were undergone, with the result that in May of this year the Battalion was pronounced "fit for service."

But the handicaps had been most severe. From the time of its arrival in Burma the Battalion had been split up into three, and for a considerable period into four, separate detachments, and stretched out over a distance of 750 miles. The difficulties of supervision, training, and administration can be imagined! In addition guard and escort duties in connection with Turkish Prisoners of War Camps at Thayetmyo, Meiktila, and Shwebo, had made a constant drain upon the numbers available for training.

The Battalion assembled at Rangoon on 16th May 1917 on transfer to India. The 3rd Garrison Battalion of the Bedfordshire Regiment relieved it at Meiktila, and a Garrison Battalion of the Royal Irish Fusiliers took its place at Shwebo. Nearly two and a half years had elapsed since its last parade as a complete unit.

Many changes were found: Major C. H. Goodland and Capt. C. Ward Jackson had been appointed to the Staff of Burma Division; Capt. H. H. Broadmead had gone to Bombay as Staff Captain; 2nd Lieut. W. S. Hearn had been transferred to the Indian Army; 2nd Lieut. J. L. Steele had become Adjutant of a Prisoners of War Camp, whilst 2nd Lieut. G. A. Vallance was officiating as Staff Captain, Rangoon Brigade. 2nd Lieut. Vallance was subsequently appointed Brigade Major of the Sialkot Cavalry Brigade.

There had been two changes of Regimental Sergeant-Majors. In March 1917 Sergeant-Major W. Cayford received a commission; a Sergeant of the Somerset Light Infantry, and the Instructor of the Williton Company of the 5th Battalion at the outbreak of war, he joined the Battalion on the eve of its departure from England and did most valuable work. His influence was of the greatest service in establishing good discipline and sound *morale*. He received an appointment on the Embarkation Staff in Mesopotamia, and retired at the end of the war with the rank of Major. Sergeant A. W. Slocombe, of Wellington, succeeded him, but for a few months only, as, with 43 men of the Battalion he was left behind at Meiktila on transfer, for medical reasons, to the 3rd Garrison Battalion of the Bedfordshire Regiment. Sergeant W. E. Fry of "D" Company was appointed to fill the vacancy. This appointment he held to the end, to the satisfaction of his Commanding Officer, and he was awarded the Meritorious Service Medal soon after demobilization.

Many N.C.O.s and men had been transferred to Signals, Mechanical Transport, and Royal Flying Corps; others had been detailed for employment on special duty at the Prisoners of War Camps, for duty at Army and Divisional Headquarters, and in ordnance and clothing depots and munition factories.

CHAPTER III*

THE MESOPOTAMIA DRAFTS

I

The Draft to the 1st Battalion Oxford and Bucks Light Infantry, August 1915

ABOUT the middle of July 1915 it was considered necessary to strengthen the British units in the Indian Division then in Mesopotamia, and Drafts were required from every British Territorial Battalion in India and Burma. The 2/5th Battalion Somerset Light Infantry was ordered to send 1 officer and 40 N.C.O.s and men. Volunteers were called for, and the list was immediately over-subscribed. Those selected embarked at Rangoon, crossed to Calcutta, and thence proceeded by train to Bombay, where a troopship was waiting to convey them to Basrah.

An unusual incident happened on embarkation at Bombay. The troops, after stowing their kit on board, were allowed to return to the town. There was some mistake in the orders given with regard to the time of sailing, and as numbers of the men were departing from the docks, this mistake was suddenly realized. The ship was to sail earlier than was understood. A non-commissioned officer of the 2/5th Somersets, being among the first to hear of the mistake, immediately ran to the dock gates to give a warning to the departing men. In fact, on his own responsibility, he gave orders to all men from the 2/5th Somersets to return at once to the ship. Many men from other regiments took no notice, and the result was that the 2/5th Somerset Light Infantry Draft was the only one out of about fifteen similar Drafts to sail with a full complement. Some of the missing men from the other regiments overtook the ship in a tug, the remainder came on by train to Karachi, where the ship called to pick them up.

On arrival at Basrah the Draft transhipped into a paddle steamer, which slowly made its way up stream to Amarah. This was for the time being the headquarters of the 6th (Poona) Division. The Draft was then distributed among the platoons of one of the companies of the 1st Battalion Oxford and Bucks Light Infantry, which was the British Battalion of the 17th (Indian) Brigade. There

* Reference map on page 76.

was some disappointment that these Drafts were not retained as units, but it was explained that to do so would upset the organization of the companies to which they were attached, and no doubt it was advantageous that the untried men of the Drafts should gain their experience side by side with the hardened men of the Oxfords.

The heat at Amarah was intense: it seemed to smite upwards from the ground, so that the protection even of helmets, spine-pads, and goggles seemed inadequate at midday. The advance, therefore, which began early in September, came as a welcome relief.

The Division quickly and without appreciable opposition moved up the Tigris, until within striking distance of the Es Sinn position, where the Turks were astride the river, and evidently intended to make a determined resistance to prevent the British reaching Kut.

After some reconnaissance, the main body of the 6th Division made a long night march on the 27th-28th September, arriving before dawn behind the left flank of the enemy's position. Meanwhile, a small force advanced up the right bank to divert attention, and to endeavour to keep that part of the enemy's force which was on the right bank of the river from crossing until the British gunboats had been able to destroy the enemy's bridge.

The main attack was delivered at the rear of the chain of redoubts on the left bank. The Oxfords carried their objective without artillery preparation, but owing to a good deal of delay in other parts of the programme, it was impossible for them immediately to follow up their success. Darkness was coming on when orders came to concentrate on the river. At this time no one knew, apparently, where were the enemy's forces, which had been holding the trenches nearer the river. In the course of their march, however, the Oxfords suddenly encountered heavy rifle fire coming out of the gathering darkness. They immediately attacked, but the enemy disappeared, and it being too dark for the position to be appreciated, the Oxfords bivouacked on the spot. The cold that night was as intense as the heat had been during the day, and clad only in khaki drill, without coats or blankets, few were able to sleep.

Next day it was realized that the enemy had escaped, and were too swift even for the cavalry. Kut was entered without difficulty.

With incidental delays and occasional reconnaissances in force, the Division made its way up river with only slight resistance until able to encamp within striking distance of the Ctesiphon position, which had then become the main Turkish defence of Baghdad. This position, as war went in Mesopotamia, was immensely strong. It consisted of a chain of redoubts, mainly on the left bank of the river, near the famous ruin called the Ctesiphon Arch.

The plan of attack was for the main part of the 6th Division to strike at the redoubt on the extreme left of the Turkish position. The 17th Brigade, to which the 2/5th Somerset Light Infantry Draft was attached, was ordered, however, to make a frontal attack nearer the river. The idea was to pin down the enemy's troops in their trenches, in the hope that they would be cut off when the main attack had succeeded.

The Division marched all night of the 21st-22nd November, and arrived within sight of the enemy's position before dawn. The 17th Brigade advanced steadily and deployed. It did not meet with very heavy fire until about a thousand yards from the enemy's wire, when it was realized that it was getting too close to the river, and the order came "Right Turn," in order to correct this mistake. This was most unfortunate, because at this moment the Oxfords had just come under very heavy shrapnel fire, which continued to cause heavy casualties until they were able to continue their advance after righting direction. As the Oxfords advanced, the rifle fire from the enemy's trenches became more and more devastating. The ground was as flat as a billiard table, with scarcely a blade of grass. When the line, much disorganized, reached a small water ditch about a hundred yards from the Turkish wire, it was obvious that the frontal attack could not be pressed home unless and until the main operation had succeeded against the enemy's left flank.

The Oxfords remained, therefore, for some time in the water ditch until they saw that the turning movement had succeeded, and the enemy's position was being rolled up from left to right. They then rushed in and captured a number of the enemy, who by that time seemed only anxious to get away.

Quickly reforming, the Oxfords attacked a line of sand-hills about two miles away to which a number of the enemy had retreated. They were so weakened, however, by casualties, that coming under a very heavy fire, they retired to the redoubt at the extreme left of the enemy's captured position. Here the Oxfords spent a quiet night, but for the first time realized the appalling nature of the casualties they had suffered. About fifty per cent. of the strength of the Battalion were either killed or wounded.

Next day, the 23rd November, and the following night, the enemy made heavy counter-attacks, which were repulsed with heavy loss to the Turks.

On the 24th orders were received to concentrate near the river. The enemy for the time being had retired, but on the 25th were reported to be heavily reinforced and returning to the attack. General Townshend, commanding the Division, having evacuated his 4,000 casualties, decided to retire. There were no other troops of consequence in Mesopotamia, and had this Division been wiped out entirely, the Turks could have dropped down stream to Basrah, and all the fruits of the campaign would have been lost. No one, therefore, can challenge the wisdom of General Townshend's decision to fall back and hold Kut, which was the key to the situation, commanding as it did the Tigris end of the only water-way which linked the Tigris with the Euphrates. It was essential to prevent the enemy from availing themselves of this alternative line of advance.

The retirement was carried out in splendid order, but was considerably harassed by the enemy, especially on the 1st December, when the Division had to fight a prolonged rear-guard action to save the transport.

The British were able, however, to dig in at Kut without much embarrassment, and although continuously sniped at and shelled, by Christmas Eve had entrenched satisfactorily the neck of the bend of the Tigris at the apex of which Kut is situated.

Upon Christmas Eve the Turks launched the only determined attack which they made during the siege. It began at dawn with an intense bombardment of an old mud fort which was held by part of the 17th Brigade, including the company of the Oxfords to which the 2/5th Somerset Light Infantry Draft was attached. The moment the bombardment ceased, the Turks launched a heavy infantry attack, gaining access to the fort in some places, but by the late afternoon had been definitely repulsed.

That night, however, as soon as the moon had risen, the attack was renewed, and continued with great ferocity throughout the night. By next morning, Christmas Day, 1915, the Turks had abandoned the attempt, having gained no foothold, and leaving the fort surrounded with thousands of their dead.

The remainder of the siege provides an interesting study of a struggle to maintain the strength of the troops, most of which were Indians, upon unaccustomed food-stuffs in rapidly diminishing quantities. Floods had to be dammed out; all manner of diseases, especially scurvy, beri-beri and fevers, dealt with; anti-aircraft guns devised, and the unforeseen situation met by all manner of craft. Although, however, the siege lasted for five months, the Turks were unwilling to face again the rough handling they received on Christmas Eve, and, apart from bombardment, they left the defenders severely alone, contenting themselves with maintaining the siege.

Meanwhile, the large relieving force advancing was meeting with heavy

THE MESOPOTAMIA DRAFTS

resistance from the Turks down stream. It soon became evident that the siege might be a long one, and rations were drastically cut down. When their great effort at the Dujaila Redoubt failed, things began to look black, and from then onwards every day was precious. The shortest possible ration was allowed which would keep the troops just able to do essential daily work. There was no longer any chance of cutting a way out, as most of the horses had been killed to limit consumption of grain, and so guns or ammunition could not be moved. Some of the younger horses and mules were, however, kept alive by feeding them on palm roots, as these remained the only source of meat.

The troops still received a small ration of very coarse bread, which by the end of the siege had been reduced to a couple of ounces a man. Sugar, butter, or fats of any kind were practically non-existent during the last month. The effect of this was to reduce even the comparatively healthy men of the garrison almost to wrecks, but the *morale* of the whole force remained remarkably robust.

Ultimately the garrison heard that the final effort for the relief had been thwarted by floods, and there being no further hope, General Townshend received orders from India to enter into negotiations for surrender. The Turks were insistent on unconditional surrender, so guns were blown up, ammunition dumped in the river, everything of military interest destroyed, and the Turks invited to walk in.

At first the attitude of the Turkish commander led the British to expect not only courtesy but also fair treatment. He expressed the greatest admiration for the British defence, and talked freely about the brotherhood of arms. For five months the garrison had been entirely cut off from the outside world, save for wireless communication and for messages and a few packages dropped in Kut by aeroplanes from down stream. For five months Kut had remained an effective check to any considerable movement of the large Turkish army then east of Baghdad. Meanwhile the large British forces had had time to reach Basrah and begin the advance which ultimately led to the conquest of Mesopotamia. It was not, therefore, until the object had been achieved, until all resources had been expended, and until there remained to the survivors of the garrison but the desire to live, that General Townshend surrendered Kut.

Any belief in Turkish chivalry was quickly disappointed. The captive Division was marched to the neighbouring camp of Shamran; the officers were separated from the men and sent to distant camps in Asia Minor. Having got rid of the British officers from whom criticism at least was expected, the Turks proceeded to march the men of the Division toward Asia Minor via Baghdad,

Mosul, and Rasalain. Considering the starved condition of the men, their lack of any proper clothing and equipment, and the complete incompetence of the Turks to organize any unexpected situation, it is no wonder that the majority died of exposure and disease. The story of the suffering of these men who, in a state of starvation, were herded by the Turks across the desert, is one which destroys all claim of the Turks to be a civilized people. That story can only adequately be told by one of those non-commissioned officers or men who had the amazing courage and physical strength to survive the ordeal.

Note

This record would not be complete without the names of the personnel of the Draft, and they are here given. A perusal of the casualties which were suffered will afford a striking commentary upon the restrained and graphic narrative which was written by the officer who commanded it, Lieut. J. S. P. Mellor.[1]

Name	Casualty
ADAMS, Private Arthur	Wounded 24.12.1915. Death presumed as having occurred while a prisoner of War in Turkey between 29.4.1916 and 26.10.1917.
ADAMS, Private Albert	Wounded 24.12.1915. Died while a prisoner of War in Turkey, 18.6.1916.
ADAMS, Corporal J.	Wounded 28.9.1915. Died at Rangoon 23.8.1917.
BANGER, Private W. G.	
BARRINGTON, Private S.	
BOWERMAN, Private E.	
BROOKS, Private A. C.	Wounded 22.11.1915.
BROWN, Private A. V.	Wounded 22-24.11.1915.
CHIDLEY, Lance-Corporal M.	
CRUICKSHANK, Private A.	Died of wounds, Mesopotamia 26.11.1915.
DURDAN, Private C.	Wounded 22-24.11.1915.
ENGLAND, Private W.	
EVANS, Private R.	
HAWKER, Private C.	

[1] Afterwards Sir John S. P. Mellor, Bart.

THE MESOPOTAMIA DRAFTS

Name	Casualty
HAWKES, Private E. E.	Wounded 22.11.1915.
HAWKINS, Private R.	Taken prisoner of War on the fall of Kut.
JENNINGS, Private C. H.	Died at Kut 25.4.1916.
JONES, Private J.	Wounded 28.9.1915.
LONG, Private C.	Died of wounds, Mesopotamia 28.11.1915.
MAHRENHOLZ, Corporal F. E.	Wounded 28.9.1915. Died at Dinapore 29.8.1917.
MALE, Private A.	
MANNING, Lance-Corporal P.	Wounded 22.11.1915 and 20.4.1916.
MANSFIELD, Private W. T.	
MELLOR, Lieutenant J. S. P.	Wounded 22.11.1915 and 24.12.1915.
MORGAN, Private R.	Wounded 25.12.1915. Died while a prisoner of War in Turkey 9.10.1916.
PIPE, Private N.	Presumed taken prisoner of War on the fall of Kut. Presumed to have died while a prisoner of War between 29.4.1916 and 31.12.1916.
RADFORD, Private G.	Wounded 7.1.1916.
REED, Lance-Corporal G.	
SHIRE, Private W.	Wounded 22.11.1915.
SHOPLAND, Private S.	Taken prisoner of War on the fall of Kut. Died while a prisoner of War 15.7.1916.
SIMPSON, Corporal A.	
SINGLETON, Private B.	Wounded 22-24.11.1915.
SLOCOMBE, Sergeant W.	Wounded 28.9.1915.
STEVENS, Private E.	Wounded 1.1.1916.
STRINGFELLOW, Private E. L.	
TANCOCK, Private S. J.	Wounded 28.9.1915, 21.12.1915, and 1.2.1916. Died of wounds 8.3.1916.
TAYLOR, Private T.	Killed in action at Kut, 21.12.1915.
THOMPSON, Private A.	Wounded in action, Mesopotamia 18.10.1915.

Name	Casualty
Turner, Private R.	Died while a prisoner of War in Turkey 12.8.1916.
Wellman, Private B.	Killed in action at Ctesiphon 22.11.1915.
Wheadon, Private G.	Wounded 28.9.1915 and 25.12.1915. Died of wounds 8.2.1916.

II

Machine Gun Section

In 1917 it was decided to form Machine Gun Companies from the Machine Gun Sections of the Regular and Territorial Battalions in India, to reinforce the Brigades on service in Mesopotamia. The Machine Gun Section of the 2/5th Battalion Somerset Light Infantry left Dinapore on 25th July for Mhow in Central India, where the Machine Gun Centre with depot had been formed. On arrival it was posted to the 256 Machine Gun Company commanded by Capt. H. G. Redman, O.B.E., 1/4th Battalion the Wiltshire Regiment. The Company was fortunate in its Commanding Officer, and, as the majority of the Sections came from West Country Units, a strong esprit de corps soon developed.

No. 256 Machine Gun Company comprised one section from each of the following: 2nd Battalion Somerset Light Infantry; 1st Battalion South Lancashire Regiment; 2/5th Battalion Somerset Light Infantry; 2/4th Battalion Somerset Light Infantry; 1/4th Battalion Wiltshire Regiment; 2/4th Battalion Wiltshire Regiment.

The 2/5th Somerset Machine Gun Section was commanded by Lieut. A. H. Armstrong, and consisted of Lieut. W. E. Hunt, Second-in-Command, Section Sergeants Richards and Grinter, and 40 other ranks. After receiving a complete issue of Vickers Machine Guns, equipment, horses and mules with their Indian drivers, the Company spent two months in training at Mhow before sailing for Basrah in the middle of October 1917. Basrah was reached towards the end of October, and the Company went into camp at Magill, not far from the Shatt al Arab. Orders were then received to proceed to Baghdad. A river paddle steamer took the Company as far as Qurnah; from Qurnah to Amarah the journey was by train, thence to Kut by steamer, and from there the Company marched to Baghdad. This was very good training, each day's march being about 15 miles, the distance between the halting stages. The route was through Aziziyah and near the famous arch of Ctesiphon. Baghdad was reached on 12th November 1917, a few days before General Maude died from cholera, a loss which was irreparable. The Company went into a Rest Camp near the Railway Station, and on the right bank of the Tigris.

Early in December orders were received to join the 50th Brigade of the 15th Indian Division, at Fallujah on the Euphrates, 40 miles west of Baghdad. The Company marched from Baghdad across the desert between the two rivers, the journey taking three days. Fallujah, a small Arab town, is situated on the right bank of the Euphrates, and is the centre of a large and cultivated area on the road to Ramadi. It was, therefore, a strategic position on the main road down the Euphrates to Baghdad. The river was crossed by a bridge of boats as at Baghdad.

Brigade training was carried out for some weeks, and the Company had some good machine gun firing practice, the undulating ground being especially suitable for indirect firing. At Fallujah the section played some very strenuous games of Rugby; Private Wyatt of Taunton was the backbone of the team, and the section, after defeating every unit which accepted its challenge, was only defeated by the whole Brigade. At this time of the year the nights were bitterly cold but during the day the sun was quite hot and the air invigorating.

At the beginning of 1918 the Turks, who were in occupation of Hit on the Euphrates, some 50 miles north of Ramadi, received reinforcements. Early in February the 50th Brigade moved up the Euphrates to a position beyond Ramadi. Later in the month orders were received to advance on Hit and drive the Turks out. A strong reconnaissance in force made from a position 10 miles south of Hit and designed to envelop the right flank of the Turkish position revealed a retiring enemy. During the night of 9th March the town of Hit was occupied.

The Brigade then moved northwards along the river to Sahiliyah. Here the country becomes much more rugged, and the formation of the ground changes to hills with deep valleys, with no cultivation other than small groups of date gardens along the fringes of the river.

In the middle of March 1918 the 15th Division was concentrated at Sahiliyah, with the intention of making a final drive against the Turks then at Khan Baghdadi, some miles north, and if possible to cut them off entirely from their northern communications south of Deir Az Zor.

On 25th March the 50th Brigade with 256 Machine Gun Company left Sahiliyah at 9 p.m., the 2/5th Somerset Machine Gun Section being with the Advance Guard. The night was bitterly cold. The Turkish outpost position was some three miles south of Khan Baghdadi. At 2 a.m. on the 26th the Advance Guard came under fire from the Turkish outpost line, and there were several casualties. Owing to the darkness and the hilly nature of the ground it was so difficult to keep in touch with other units that it was found necessary to halt until early dawn, when the troops were able to reform for the attack on the main position. Most of the Brigade took cover under the hills.

The attack on the main Turkish position commenced about 9 a.m. The advance was made under shell fire over a distance of two miles across a wide valley. The Turks were holding trenches on the crest of the hills facing south. At 5 p.m. the attack was pushed home up the hills with the bayonet, No. 256 Machine Gun Company being on the extreme left of the 50th Brigade, giving covering fire and moving forward as opportunity offered. The Cavalry Brigade and armoured cars during the night had, after a long and difficult march, worked round the Turkish flank to the Aleppo Road, where it crossed the Wadi Hauran, and cut off the enemy's retreat by road and river. The attempt of the Turks to break through in the night was repulsed, and next morning the pursuit was continued by the leading Brigade and several thousands were captured with 14 guns, 50 machine guns, together with the Turkish Divisional commander and his staff. The armoured cars and cavalry pressed on and captured Haditha on the 27th and Ana on the 28th. These operations practically completed the break-up of the Turkish Forces on the Euphrates, the armoured cars having proceeded 70 miles north of Ana, and finally disposed of any threat from the intended Turco-German army that was to have descended from Aleppo to recapture Baghdad.

In an order of the day issued on the 28th March 1918 Major-General Andrews, commanding the 50th Brigade, expressed his profound admiration for the splendid qualities of endurance and fortitude under most trying conditions. " To be continuously under arms, marching and attacking for 35 hours with little food and very little water and to have, during that period, carried out these attacks, the last of which was against a position with many machine guns, is a feat of which we may be justly proud."

After these operations the Company moved back to camp at Sahiliyah, and later on to Hit. At the beginning of May 1918 Kifri and Kurkuk were taken with several thousand prisoners, and in November the 17th and 18th Divisions took Mosul just as the Armistice was signed, and the whole of Mesopotamia was cleared of the Turks. Lieut. A. H. Armstrong was invalided out of Mesopotamia in September of 1918 and returned to the Machine Gun depot at Mhow. Lieut.

W. E. Hunt was seconded in 1918 for duty with the political service and continued so employed until 1922. After the Armistice the Company was joined with others into a Machine Gun Battalion for demobilization.

Sergeant Frampton, who had taken the place of Sergeant Richards, appointed to a Commission in the I.A.R.O., was accidentally shot in the Machine Gun depot at Mhow in 1919.

CHAPTER IV

INDIA

THE Battalion which had sailed from Rangoon on 17th May 1917, escorted by H.M.A.S. "Psyche," disembarked at Calcutta on 20th May. It had been posted to the Presidency Brigade of the 8th Lucknow Division. Headquarters, with "A" and "B" Companies, at once entrained for Dinapore, a long-established cantonment on the banks of the Ganges, some ten miles from the City of Patna, the Headquarters of the Government of Bihar and Orissa.

The country was flat, highly cultivated, and densely populated, and the climate moist and trying. Opportunities for field training were much restricted by the nature of the surroundings, but as no other British troops were stationed in the whole Province, the population of which was over 30,000,000, chiefly Hindus, the strategic importance of the station was considerable.

"C" Company went to Barrackpore on the River Hooghly, about fifteen miles up stream from Calcutta. "D" Company became the garrison of Dum Dum, some seven miles nearer Calcutta, and in both these detachments guard duties were extremely heavy. They included the protection of the rifle factory at Ishapore, the arsenal at Dum Dum, and the gun factory at Cossipore. In each station training ground was very limited and few men were available for parades. Thus in India, as in Burma, the Battalion was denied an opportunity of training as a complete unit, although this handicap was lessened to some extent by an annual camp in the cold weather.

Three hot weathers spent in the plains of Burma and India had affected the health of the Battalion to such an extent that as many men as possible were sent to the hill stations of Lebong and Jalapahar during the hot weather, and Lieut.-Colonel J. R. Paull took over the duties of Commandant at Jalapahar. At the end of July the Battalion received reinforcements from England of 250 other ranks; these and smaller parties which followed in the autumn were duly posted to the different companies. The new men, though not all of Somerset stock, were excellent material, and soon took their place in their new surroundings.

On 30th May Private H. C. Fudge died of cholera at Dinapore. This was the only casualty due to that terrible disease which was suffered by the Battalion during its whole period of service in the East.

At the end of September the garrison of Dinapore consisted only of Battalion Headquarters, a few officers who had recently arrived from England and approximately 100 men. It was at this time that the Mohamedan festival known as the Bakhr'Id was celebrated. As the Mohamedans claim the right on this occasion to sacrifice a cow and the cow is sacred to the Hindus, trouble between the adherents of the two religions is always to be anticipated, and all troops were confined to barracks in expectation of an outbreak of rioting.

At the commencement of October a report was received from the civil authorities of Dinapore that serious fighting had occurred between Mohamedans and Hindus at Arrah, fifty miles distant from Dinapore, and that the police had been compelled to open fire. They asked for the immediate despatch of the largest possible force available to quell the disturbance.

Major W. H. Speke, who was at this time commanding the Battalion at Dinapore, at once detailed a force consisting of 2 officers and 70 men under the command of the Adjutant, Capt. T. M. Pulman, the only officer at Dinapore with experience of the country. This party left Dinapore Railway Station, four miles from Cantonments, within two hours of the call, and reached Arrah after dark. Here the local magistrate explained that the trouble was caused by parties of Hindus, several thousand strong, collecting together, attacking the isolated Mohamedan communities in the villages around, killing and destroying. The force established its headquarters at Jagdispur in the centre of the disturbed area, about ten miles from railhead. Rations were sent up daily from Battalion Headquarters, but, on account of the hot weather, the meat usually arrived unfit for consumption, and local arrangements had to be made for feeding the troops. There the force remained for nearly three weeks, constantly sending out small Columns, usually consisting of 1 officer and 20 other ranks, in response to urgent calls from neighbouring villages for protection. This entailed long forced marches over soft dusty roads in the heat of an Indian summer. Unfortunately it was often found that the call had come too late, for the rioters had arrived first, destroyed life and property, and disappeared. Sometimes, however, the Column reached the village in time; on one such occasion it was confronted by a mob of about 5,000 excited Hindus, bent on destruction. After all efforts on the part of the magistrate had failed to stop their advance, 2nd Lieut. Revell, who was in command, was obliged to open fire to prevent his little party from being overwhelmed.

A force of cavalry and several battalions of Military Police were sent to the district to assist the Infantry, but still the trouble spread, and Major Speke, who in the meantime had been reinforced by 2 officers and 307 men of the Battalion from the hills, was called upon to despatch further parties, both to the Arrah district and to Gaya, about fifty miles to the south. These measures had the ultimate effect of quelling the disturbances, and after the lapse of five weeks the troops were recalled to Dinapore. The only casualty was Private E. Binding, who was accidentally shot at Gaya.

The Arrah riots exemplified one of the most difficult problems in Indian administration, the calling out of troops in aid of the civil power.

During the summer of this year the Battalion Machine Gunners with their officers, Lieut. A. H. Armstrong and 2nd Lieut. W. E. Hunt, were transferred to the Machine Gun Depot at Mhow, preparatory to service in Mesopotamia, and the Signallers were transferred to the Wessex Divisional Signals in Mesopotamia. The Battalion also lost Lieut. Lord St. Audries, transferred to England, Lieut. R. O. Hobhouse, who proceeded to Egypt for training as a pilot in the Royal Flying Corps, in which he subsequently saw much active service in France, and 2nd Lieut. John Fowler attached to Headquarters Burma Division as Physical Training Officer.

Several N.C.O.s and men also left the Battalion, having been given commissions in the Indian Army. Of these, Sergeant W. G. Bailey, who whilst serving with his Indian Regiment the 1/72nd Punjabis in Palestine and Egypt in 1918 and 1919, won the M.C. at the Battle of Et Tireh on 19th September 1918. Sergeant C. Pattemore of Crewkerne, who died at Calcutta in August of this year was a distinct loss to "C" Company; of happy disposition and sterling character, he was greatly liked by both officers and men.

In October a further party consisting of Sergeant W. A. Medlicott, 1 corporal and 20 privates left the Battalion on transfer to No. 264 Machine Gun Company at Mhow. Later, this party formed a sub-section of No. 270 Machine Gun Company, and in January 1918 went to Quetta. Here—in the 4th Division— the Company took part in the operations against the Marri tribes, and in 1919 it saw service in the Afghan War. It proceeded to Chaman and took part in the assault of Spinbaldock Fort on 27th May.

In January 1918 the monotony of garrison duty was agreeably varied by the Brigade Camp at Madhupur, on the borders of Bihar and Bengal. Some 520 officers and men of the Battalion were present. Field firing and tactical operations were carried out under most favourable conditions. Officers and men showed the utmost energy and keenness, and such a high standard was attained that the Brigade-Commander, Brigadier-General Strange, caused a Demonstration Platoon to be formed for the instruction of other units. Kitchener's Test was passed with credit, and at the conclusion General Strange complimented the Battalion on the work that had been done.

The firing of the musketry course in this year showed still further improvement. In June "D" and "C" Companies at Dum Dum and Barrackpore were relieved by "A" and "B" Companies respectively. Detachments were sent from time to time to Lebong and Jalapahar, and Lieut.-Colonel J. R. Paull took over the command at Lebong from June to August. During this year Capt. W. Winter Goode, who had commanded "D" Company from its formation, left on transfer to Lucknow as Station Staff Officer. "D" Company also lost Company-Sergeant-Major F. G. Pilton, a most experienced and conscientious Warrant officer, who died of apoplexy in May.

The call on the Battalion for N.C.O.s and men for special duty became still more insistent in 1918. In addition to those required for duty at Army and Divisional Headquarters and in Ordnance Departments in India, many went to the Supply and Transport Corps and the Railway and Inland Water services of Mesopotamia. Others were attached to units of the Indian Defence Force as Instructors. A marked feature was the number of N.C.O.s sent to newly raised units of Indian Infantry for duty as Sergeant Instructors. On 7th November no less than 11 Sergeants and acting Sergeants of the Battalion left Calcutta for Mesopotamia attached to the 3/9th Bhopal Infantry. Internal organization was further complicated by the transfer to Garrison Battalions of men no longer fit for active service, and the receipt from these units of a number of other ranks who had recovered from the effect of wounds received during the earlier years of the War.

In September 1918 serious riots broke out in the suburbs of Calcutta, when large mobs of Moslems attempted to march into the city to take part in a mass meeting which the Governor of Bengal had prohibited. Picquets were ordered to proceed from Barrackpore and Dum Dum to Fort William at a moment's notice, and on arrival were sent out in taxi-cabs to points where special danger threatened. One such picquet, under the command of Lieut. J. Bell, was confronted in the suburb of Garden Reach by an excited crowd of over 3,000 rioters who had already made a murderous assault upon a British mill manager. Police officers attempted in vain to turn the mob back, and it was not until a shower of stones had been followed by an attack at close quarters by fanatical Mohamedans armed with lathis (bamboo poles tipped with lead or iron) that the party was compelled to open fire. The casualties at point-blank range were heavy, but the effect was instantaneous, the crowd melted away as if by magic, and when news of the affair reached Calcutta the disturbances which had broken out in other quarters, involving some loss of life, ceased immediately. The leading Calcutta paper (*The Statesman*) in commenting upon the riots said: "There can be no question as to the justification of the action of the troops. If a mob, several thousand strong, fired by fanaticism, had swarmed across the Calcutta Maidan and forced their way into the city, a situation of the utmost gravity would have arisen."

Five officers were appointed to permanent commissions in the Indian Army towards the end of this year, Capt. A. M. P. Luscombe and Lieut. C. F. B. Pearce joining the 2/17th (Punjab) Infantry, Lieuts. R. C. H. Riddell and C. N. Price the 2/76th (Punjab) Infantry, and 2nd Lieut. G. N. Martin the 1/123rd Regiment. After three years' service as Adjutant, Capt. T. M. Pulman took over command of "B" Company in November and was succeeded by Lieut. J. Bell.

During the autumn and winter an influenza epidemic swept over India with unprecedented severity, and the Battalion did not remain unscathed; admissions to hospital increased greatly and there were several deaths. At Barrackpore and Dum Dum so many men were sick that at times sentries had to be on duty for three nights out of four.

When the news of the Armistice reached the Battalion it was celebrated with the greatest joy and relief, tempered only by regret that circumstances had denied those who had volunteered for Active Service four years before the opportunity they had so keenly desired. A trying period now began; many of the original Battalion were yet to remain for nearly a year in India, awaiting demobilization, though all ranks were eager to return to the homes and families from which they had been so long separated. In spite, however, of their disappointment, their spirit remained cheerful and the discipline of the whole Battalion was as admirable during its fifth year of service as it had been hitherto.

In January 1919 a camp was held at Jasideh in Bengal where field firing and tactical operations were again the chief activities. The number able to attend, however, was small. Only a few men of "A" Company could be spared from the Dum Dum Garrison and, owing to the severity of the influenza epidemic "B" Company was not present.

During camp the first group for demobilization left for England. Lieut. J. Bell, who was included in this party, was succeeded as Adjutant by Lieut. A. E. J. Gawler.

The general unrest which spread over India during the early months of 1919, together with the operations in Afghanistan, made it impossible to continue the process of demobilization, which was proceeding so rapidly from the nearer theatres of war, except in a few very special cases. The natural disappointment was tempered by the knowledge that the need of India for British soldiers at this time was paramount, and the stress of waiting for relief was borne with patience.

Lieut. A. E. J. Gawler was demobilized for civil employment in India in August, and his place as Adjutant was taken by Lieut. G. H. Dickinson.

In September orders were issued by Army Headquarters in India that all men who had enlisted or were serving in 1914 were, if they so desired, to be returned to England for demobilization immediately transport was available. As was only to be expected all expressed their desire to return at the earliest opportunity, and on 18th October these 1914 men to the number of about 200 were despatched to the concentration camp at Deolali.

Meanwhile Battalion Headquarters, with "C" and "D" Companies, were relieved at Dinapore and on 8th September proceeded to Fort William, Calcutta. Here, some ten days later, they were joined by "A" Company from Dum Dum; but "B" Company at Barrackpore was not relieved until the second week in October.

During the early part of October all ranks then serving with the Battalion who had enlisted after January 1916 were sent to the 2nd Battalion Somerset Light Infantry, then stationed at Peshawar. The number of N.C.O.s and men in this category was about 150. It is interesting to record that most of them saw active service in the operations on the North West Frontier with the 2nd Battalion.

On the day after the 1914 men had left for Deolali, orders were received that the remainder of the Battalion, then reduced almost to a skeleton, would proceed to England on the troopship "Nevasa," due to sail almost immediately, there being accommodation for a small party of this size on the ship.

Consequently the Battalion, consisting of 13 officers and 132 other ranks, left Fort William on 21st October for Bombay. Lieut.-Colonel J. R. Paull, Major W. H. Speke, Capt. T. M. Pulman, and Capt. and Quartermaster T. H. Hood were the only officers then returning who had left England with the Battalion nearly five years previously.

The 1914 men saw to their chagrin the Battalion troop train passing through Deolali *en route* to Bombay; and thus it came about that those men who had been the first to join were the last to return. However, their ship followed closely upon the "Nevasa," and their return was not long delayed. The following farewell message was received from His Excellency the Commander-in-Chief in India.

SIMLA,
27th October 1919.

Officers, Warrant Officers, Non-Commissioned Officers and Men of the 2/5th Battalion (Prince Albert's) Somerset Light Infantry.

On your departure from India I desire to place on record my high appreciation of your services to the Empire during the period of the Great War.

Many of you, previous to the outbreak of War, had, by joining the Territorial Force, already given proofs of that patriotism and public spirit for which the Force has rendered itself so conspicuous.

On the declaration of War your ranks were quickly filled by eager volunteers, animated by the same spirit of self-sacrifice. When called upon to undertake the further obligation of service overseas your response was immediate and unanimous. By so doing you set free a large number of regular units for service in the main theatres of War, at a time when every trained soldier was of the greatest value.

I share with you the disappointment, which I know you all feel so keenly, that it has not been your lot to fight the Enemy in Europe. Many of you, however, have seen service on the Indian Frontier and by your conduct and bearing have added to the reputation of the famous regiments whose names you bear.

For the greater portion of your service in India you have been engaged in the somewhat dull routine of garrison duty. The standard of efficiency which you have attained, both in training for War and in discipline, reflects the highest credit on you all.

Since the termination of active fighting in all the theatres of War you have been subjected to the further stress of waiting for your relief. That you have appreciated the difficulties which the authorities have had to face in this respect is clear from the patience with which you have borne this trying period.

You are now returning to your homes in the United Kingdom and I bid you good-bye, God speed, and a happy homecoming.

As an old Commander of a Territorial Division at home I am proud to have again been associated with this Force in India.

(Signed) C. C. MONRO (General),
Commander-in-Chief in India.

INDIA

So large a part do athletics play in the life of a Regiment in India that no apology is needed for placing on record the doings of the representative teams of the Battalion during its service in the East.

The enthusiasm shown for Rugby Football was so great that games were played even in the most unseasonable climatic conditions, and on the roughest of grounds. The Regimental XV, composed largely of members of the Bridgwater, North Petherton, Taunton, and Wellington Clubs, won the Burma Cup in 1916, defeating in the Final the 1/4th Battalion The Border Regiment.

In 1918 it followed the example of the 1/5th Battalion by winning that most coveted of all the Army Rugby Trophies in India—The Calcutta Cup. In the final round the team was captained by Corporal W. Knight, and its opponents were the 1st Battalion Duke of Wellington's (West Riding Regiment) who were beaten by eight points to nil.

This success was repeated in 1919 when, as holders, it defeated the 1/4th Battalion The Border Regiment in the semi-finals by 15 points to 3, and the 1st Brecknockshire Battalion The South Wales Borderers in the final round by 8 points to 5. Sergeant G. Davidge was the captain of the team.

At Association Football, always very popular in a West Country Regiment, lack of practice as a side prevented the XI doing itself justice. However, in 1917 it reached the semi-final round of the All India Cup, and it took part with considerable success in the various League Competitions.

Due mainly to the skill and knowledge possessed by Capt. C. Ward Jackson, Horsemanship was fostered to a marked degree, and whilst the Battalion was stationed in Burma a reputation was gained for the high standard of riding of several of its officers.

Polo was played regularly at Meiktila and Shwebo, and the officers' team of Capt. Ward Jackson's Company was successful in Polo Tournaments at Mandalay and Maymyo. In the last named it met and defeated a Burma Military Police Team which was mounted on the very ponies which Capt. Ward Jackson's team had collected and trained for the occasion, but had been compelled to sell to the Police as the Battalion was under orders for transfer to India.

Hockey was played with much keenness and the team would undoubtedly have done well in any competition.

Conditions were not favourable for the playing of cricket to any extent.

The "Nevasa" reached Plymouth on 16th November where the Battalion disembarked and entrained for Sandling, near Folkestone. After a stay here of two days, the Cadre, consisting of the Commanding Officer, the Adjutant, and the Quartermaster, with 50 other ranks, proceeded to Taunton, whilst the remainder went to Fovant for demobilization.

At Taunton Lieut.-Colonel J. R. Paull and the Cadre received an official Welcome Home from the Mayor, Alderman H. J. Van Trump, and leading citizens of the town. At the luncheon which followed a warm tribute was paid to the services rendered by the Battalion during its five years' absence overseas.

CHAPTER V

DISBANDMENT

FOR several weeks after the return of the Cadre, officers who had been extra regimentally employed, others who had left the Battalion on being granted Commissions in the Indian Army, and small parties of N.C.O.s and men arrived home for demobilization. They returned from Persia, China, the North West Frontier, as well as from Mesopotamia, India, and Burma.

Capt. and Quartermaster T. H. Hood with Orderly Room Colour-Sergeant F. W. Berry, and a small party stayed on at the Territorial Hall, Taunton, to wind up the affairs of the Battalion. Much had to be done, and it was not until 25th February 1920 that the 2/5th Battalion officially ceased to exist. Colour-Sergeant Berry was one of the first to join the Battalion and the last to leave it. His Commanding Officer and the Adjutants under whom he served place on record their appreciation of his quiet, accurate, and resourceful work. He was imperturbable, never tired, and nothing was too much trouble for him.

The spirit of courage and leadership which had been fostered in the Battalion from its earliest days found expression in the active service which those officers, who, in November 1918, had taken up permanent commissions in the Indian Army, experienced on the North West Frontier in 1919 and succeeding years. It was during the operations in Waziristan that Capt. R. C. H. Riddell was killed. His Battalion, the 2/76th Punjabis, formed part of the Derajat Column, to the advance of which the Mahsuds offered very stubborn resistance at Ahnai Tanzi, Waziristan, on 14th January 1920. Capt. Riddell was in the firing line with his Company. Encouraged by his example of coolness and fearlessness against the fierce attacks of the enemy, his men won their way to the hill-top, the possession of which was vital to the safety of the Column below. But at the cost of his own life—for during the afternoon Capt. Riddell was struck in the neck by a bullet and died an hour or two later. Capt. Riddell was a most promising officer, and greatly beloved by his men.

His friend and companion Capt. C. N. Price, who had joined the 2/5th

Battalion with him in the early days of the War, also fought in this action. For his gallant conduct he was awarded the M.C.

Capt. A. M. P. Luscombe and Lieut. C. F. B. Pearce also saw much service in these operations, whilst Capt. H. H. Broadmead served on the Staff of the 43rd Indian Infantry Brigade in the South Waziristan Expedition of 1917, and in the Afghan War of 1919; as D.A.A. and Q.M.G. of the Bannu Force he took part in the Mahsud campaign of 1919, being mentioned in despatches.

On 27th March 1920 a King's Colour was presented by Major F. M. E. Kennedy, C.B., on behalf of the Army Council, and handed over to Lieut.-Colonel J. R. Paull and the officers of the Battalion.

The occasion was a reunion for all ranks of the 1/5th, 2/5th, 3/5th Battalions, and was held at the Territorial Hall, Taunton. There was an attendance of over 200. It was appropriate that this opportunity was taken to outline the plans for the reconstitution of the Territorial Army in Somerset, and to announce the selection of Lieut.-Colonel D. S. Watson, D.S.O., T.D., who had served with the 1/5th Battalion throughout the War, to command the newly formed 5th Battalion.

Major Kennedy explained that His Majesty had authorized the presentation of a Flag to every Battalion in the Army raised for the duration of the War that had served overseas, and that the Colour for the 2/5th Battalion had been received only two days before. His instructions were to present it to the Commanding Officer of the Battalion, but as Lieut.-Colonel Paull was unfortunately unable to be present, he had been authorized to hand it over to Major C. H. Goodland who helped to raise the Battalion in 1914, and accompanied it overseas. Its resting place lay with the officers, but it must be consecrated, and deposited in some sacred or public building in the district, as it could not become the property of any individual. "I am sure," Major Kennedy concluded, "that this King's Colour which means so much in the British Army will be respected and honoured by every officer, N.C.O., and man who served in the 2/5th Battalion, and I have much pleasure in handing it over to you."

Major Goodland received the Colour. In reply, he assured Major Kennedy that it would be held by all who had served with the 2/5th Battalion as a mark of the King's appreciation of their services, and cherished by them as a symbol of the devotion of those members who fought, and suffered, and laid down their lives.

In the early autumn—on 9th September 1920—the King's Colour of the 2/5th Battalion Somerset Light Infantry was consecrated in the Parish Church of St. Mary, Ilminster, and laid up with befitting ceremonial. This Church had

DISBANDMENT

been chosen by the officers as a suitable resting place because Ilminster was the centre of the district from which the Battalion was raised in 1914, and was the home of its Commanding Officer and Second-in-Command, both of whom had served with it from its earliest days to its disbandment. There was a large congregation, including Lieut.-Colonel Paull, Major Speke, and many officers and men of the old Battalion, as well as Colonel E. F. Cooke-Hurle and officers of the 1/5th Battalion.

The Colour Party, consisting of Capt. F. E. Spurway, carrying the Colour, and Company-Sergeant-Majors Ewens, Slocombe, and West, was met at the west door by the vicar, Rev. Prebendary Street, and conducted to the chancel steps. Rev. Leslie Newton, Chaplain to the Forces, read the lesson and subsequent prayers, after which the Colour Party advanced to the altar. Here the vicar received the Colour and placed it upon the altar. Bugle Major Hughes then sounded the Last Post. The vicar addressed the congregation, and promised that the Colour would be given a suitable place of honour within the church.

* * * * * *

And there the Colour rests—in the safe keeping of the vicar and churchwardens—a lasting witness to the existence of the Battalion. It hangs from the wall at the eastern end of the south aisle, and attached to the pole is a bronze plate with this inscription:

THE KING'S COLOUR
of the
2/5TH BATTALION
THE PRINCE ALBERT'S SOMERSET LIGHT INFANTRY
Formed 1914   Disbanded 1920
Served overseas throughout the Great War

HONOURS AND REWARDS

MENTION IN DESPATCHES

BROADMEAD, Lieutenant H. H.
HUNT, Lieutenant W. E.
PAULL, Lieutenant-Colonel J. R., O.B.E., T.D.

BROUGHT TO THE NOTICE OF GOVERNMENT OF INDIA FOR VALUABLE SERVICES RENDERED IN INDIA

GOODLAND, Captain C. H., T.D.
HOOD, Quartermaster and Captain T.

REWARDS

O.B.E.

PAULL, Lieutenant-Colonel J. R.

M.C.

BAILEY, Lieutenant W. G., 1/72nd Punjabis (late Sergeant 2/5th Battalion).
PRICE, Captain C. N., 2/76th Punjabis (late 2/5th Battalion).

M.S.M.

DYER, Company-Quartermaster-Sergeant Roy.
FRY, Regimental-Sergeant-Major W.

EPILOGUE

THE history of the 5th Somerset Light Infantry is one of small beginnings and great ends. Who would have thought that the 2nd V.B. Somerset Light Infantry, originally raised in 1882 by Colonel Patton, badly armed, standing alone, and only partially trained, could have reached such efficiency or attained such devotion to duty! Fortunate for England was it that she had not entirely neglected the old saw, " si vis pacem para bellum."

But whatever may be said of him otherwise, we have to thank Lord Haldane for co-ordinating our military units of the various arms into Territorial divisions. The gallantry of the war-time 5th Somerset Light Infantry has been great and the roll of honour a long one. They left a splendid example to the men of the present 5th Battalion Somerset Light Infantry, their offspring.

Dulce et decorum est pro patria mori.

William Gifford.

Honorary Colonel,
5th Bn. S.L.I.

5TH BATTALION THE SOMERSET LIGHT INFANTRY
(PRINCE ALBERT'S)

ROLL OF OFFICERS
FROM
1920 ONWARDS

ROLL OF OFFICERS

COMMANDING OFFICERS

Name	From	To
Lieut.-Col. D. S. Watson, D.S.O., T.D.	16.2.20	28.8.23
Bt.-Col. R. E. Gifford, T.D.	29.8.23	13.3.28
Lieut.-Col. W. O. Gibbs	14.3.28	

ADJUTANTS

Name	From	To
Captain E. S. GOODLAND, M.C.	16.2.20	2.6.20
Major (Bt. Lieut.-Col.) V. B. THURSTON	3.6.20	3.6.23
Captain E. H. C. FRITH, M.B.E.	3.6.23	7.6.26
Captain J. B. TAYLOR	8.6.26	13.9.28
Captain G. H. COLE	14.9.28	

QUARTERMASTERS

Name	From	To
Captain T. BOND	16.2.20	13.11.25
Lieut. C. R. DAVIS	18.2.26	

ROLL OF OFFICERS

MEDICAL OFFICERS ATTACHED TO THE BATTALION

Date of Joining	Rank on Joining	Name	Date of Leaving	Rank on Leaving
14.12.26	Lieut.	L. P. Marshall, M.C., M.B.		
7. 5.27	Lieut.	L. N. Jackson, M.C., M.B.		
29.12.28	Lieut.	A. L. Crockford, M.C.		

CHAPLAINS ATTACHED TO THE BATTALION

28. 4.28 Rev. F. E. Spurway [1]

---

[1] First commissioned in the Battalion 3.10.14; served as combatant officer with 2/5th Battalion throughout the War.

OFFICERS GAZETTED TO THE BATTALION

Name	Rank on joining and date		Rank on leaving and date	
WATSON,[1] D. S.	Lieut.	1. 4.08	Lieut.-Col.	28.8.23
GIFFORD,[2] R. E.	2nd Lieut.	1. 4.08	Brevet-Col.	13.3.28
GOODLAND, C. H.	2nd Lieut.	1. 4.08	Major	2.6.28
CALWAY, F. H. F.	2nd Lieut.	1. 5.11	Captain	10.6.25
BLAKE,[3] J. H.	2nd Lieut.	15. 1.13		
GOODLAND, E. S.	2nd Lieut.	2. 9.14	Major	2.6.20
CLARKE, G. P.	2nd Lieut.	4.12.14		
ELDER, S. H.	2nd Lieut.	4.12.14		
WARE,[4] J. R.	2nd Lieut.	13. 3.15		
FRENCH, C. L. R.	Lieut.	27.10.20	Lieut.	29.11.22
PURCHASE, R. G.	Lieut.	31.12.20	Lieut.	14. 3.23
MITCHELL, L. J. C.	2nd Lieut.	10. 3.21	Lieut.	6. 9.26
DALE, A. J.	Lieut.	19. 3.21		
GOULD, J. A.	2nd Lieut.	9. 4.21		
TRENCHARD, C.	Lieut.	21.10.21	Lieut.	8. 2.27
BYERS, B. D.	2nd Lieut.	3. 2.22	Lieut.	27. 1.28
WHITWORTH, H.	Lieut.	15.11.23	Lieut.	10. 1.28
BANWELL, J. A.	Lieut.	5. 7.24		
MARR, R. J. W.	Lieut.	6. 7.24		
BESLEY, R. G. P.	2nd Lieut.	24.11.25		
MITCHELL, R. A. H.	2nd Lieut.	27.11.25		
BRUFORD, E. J.	2nd Lieut.	28.11.25		
DANIEL, L. S.	2nd Lieut.	20.10.26		
SEALEY, J.	2nd Lieut.	20.10.26	2nd Lieut.	5.11.27
ASHFORD, A. M.	2nd Lieut.	8.12.26		
HIRST, C. W.	2nd Lieut.	9. 2.27		

[1] First commissioned in 2nd Vol. Bn. Somerset L.I. 23.9.1896; served as Lieutenant in South African War, 1900-1902 with the Volunteer Active Service Company.

[2] First commissioned in 2nd Vol. Bn. Somerset L.I. 4.11.05.

[3] On T.A. Reserve from end of war to 5.11.24, when transferred to Active List with seniority next below Capt. Dale.

[4] Served with 4th Wilts during war—rejoined 1.7.20.

ROLL OF OFFICERS

Name	Rank on joining and date	Rank on leaving and date
POLLARD, G. J.	2nd Lieut. 23. 3.27	
MOORE, F.	2nd Lieut. 3. 7.27	
RUSSELL, R. A.	2nd Lieut. 23.11.27	
KITE, C. M. B.	2nd Lieut. 28. 1.28	
GIBBS, W. O.	Lieut.-Col. 14. 3.28	
STISTED, H. G. G. H.	2nd Lieut. 27. 6.28	
TURNER, R. J. D.	2nd Lieut. 28. 7.28	
MATHER, G. R.	Lieut. 29.11.28	
WINGFIELD, R. G.	2nd Lieut. 2. 4.29	

LONDON: CHARLES WHITTINGHAM AND GRIGGS (PRINTERS), LTD.
CHISWICK PRESS, TOOKS COURT, CHANCERY LANE.

Printed in the United Kingdom
by Lightning Source UK Ltd.
113575UKS00001B/127-130